Something Beautiful

Something Beautiful

Linda Light Strasheim
with Evelyn Bence

Illustrated by Del Strasheim

Zondervan Books
Zondervan Publishing House
Grand Rapids, Michigan

SOMETHING BEAUTIFUL

This is a Zondervan Book published by the Zondervan Publishing House, 1415 Lake Drive, S.E., Grand Rapids, Michigan 49506

Library of Congress Cataloging in Publication Data

Strasheim, Linda Light.
    Something beautiful.

        1. Strasheim, Linda Light. 2. Christian biography—United States. 3. Multiple sclerosis—Patients—United States—Biography. I. Bence, Evelyn, 1952–   . II. Title.
BR1725.S834A37   1985   248.8'6'0924   [B]   84–29109
ISBN 0-310-29391-X

Edited by Kathy Heetderks
Designed by Ann Cherryman

Printed in the United States of America

86   87   88   89   90 / 9   8   7   6   5   4

Contents

Something Beautiful

Something beautiful, something good—
All my confusion He understood;
All I had to offer Him was brokenness and strife,
But He made something beautiful of my life.

If there ever were dreams that were lofty and
*   noble,*
They were my dreams at the start;
And the hopes for life's best were the hopes that I
*   harbored*
Down deep in my heart;
But my dreams turned to ashes,
My castles all crumbled,
My fortune turned to loss,
So I wrapped it all in the rags of my life,
And laid it at the cross!

—Gloria Gaither

Foreword

Beauty . . . Success . . . Self-assurance. . . .

Those three words promise—and deliver—the thrill of victory.

The young, the strong, the beautiful—such people have a natural edge in competition, and they often win with great gusto.

But what happens when the winning stops, when merely entering a room prompts stares of incredulity rather than admiration, when friends walk out?

Young, strong, and beautiful, Linda Light once had it all—beauty, success, self-assurance, and, when the world revolved around her, she, like many others in her situation, didn't seem to need God. Her days were filled with work that she loved and with meeting goals that she viewed as worthy; her evenings were full of laughter, light-heartedness, and the attentions of desirable companions.

But when her world became an ugly, empty pit, God, who had been waiting for her, reached down and scooped her into His enfolding, loving arms.

What is her condition now? Full of more peace than she ever dreamed possible. In a recent conversation she described herself as having a rags-to-riches story.

"But, Linda," I said, "that's not what it looks like. It looks more like a riches-to-rags, I-once-could-walk-but-now-I-can't story."

A questioning look came over her face but was instantly replaced by laughter. "It may look like that to a casual observer, but it surely isn't the way I see it—and I'm the one who lived it. I'm ten thousand times better off now than I was twenty years ago. Then I was sitting on top of the world; now I'm sitting in the center of Jesus' lap."

Linda's story has inspired me once again to look at life from God's perspective. He sees individuals—each one unique, and each one needy—not pretty or less-than-pretty faces, and He delights in making something beautiful of each of us, no matter who or where or what we are.

Evelyn Bence

Introduction

Out-of-town visitors always prompt out-of-the-or-dinary adventures. Last Sunday's guest was no exception. After dinner, my husband, Del, suggested that we take our visitor on a long, meandering drive around the city, and within minutes he had delivered the three of us to our first stop, a beautiful terraced garden not far from our home. Del turned the car off. Quickly and efficiently, he opened the back hatch, lifted out and unfolded my chair, and wheeled it to my side of the car. He steadied me as I pulled myself out of the passenger's seat and plunked into my ever-present mobile home—my wheelchair.

The newly planted annuals needed another week of perfect June days before they would fill out and blanket the damp tilled dirt with foliage and blossoms. As we walked—and wheeled—leisurely around the maze of sidewalks and breathed in the first breezes of summer, two little girls eyed us from afar. Then they headed our way. With shoeless feet they marched single-file between two rows of impatiens, leaving miniature inch-deep footprints in the dirt behind them.

They walked up to me, and, with a boldness they would surely lose as they grew older, each one inquired, as if the other had not asked, what was wrong with me.

Greeting them with a pleasant smile, I answered twice, as clearly as I could: "I was sick. My legs don't work. But they don't hurt me, and I'm doing okay now." I did not want to plant the seeds of nightmares in their young minds. I wanted to assure them their next sniffle would not affect their legs.

The younger girl, a blonde, who had been the leader of the flower-garden parade, reminded me of myself at her age—in the middle of, if not the cause of, the action. She was more inquisitive and less inhibited than her sister. She stood as close to my chair as she could, and just to make sure she had correctly understood my slow and somewhat muffled voice, she asked me again, "You can't walk?"

"No," I said softly.

Her face grew sad at the same time it lit up with a solution to my dilemma: "Well, then, I'll help you," and with that, she grabbed the hand-wheel and gave me a little push along the walk.

In a few moments she and her sister said goodby and ran off—back to their world where legs hold the weight of the bodies to which they're joined; back to the world where freedom means running around a baseball diamond to the cheers of your teammates or skipping through the back door of the house with an afternoon's catch of fish flung over your shoulder; back to the carefree world of childhood I remember so well.

1 *Land of Oz*

No one in her right mind would have dreamed of escaping "over the rainbow" from the Kansas of my childhood; to me it was as colorful as the Land of Oz was to Dorothy. There was nothing black-and-white about the quiet residential streets of Topeka, and Duncan Drive lacked nothing but traffic.

Play filled my days and dreams. My dad and the neighborhood boys filled my roster of play-mates—*Who wants to spend time with sisters anyway?* I thought. *With girls?* If Dad was home and I awake, we were together—fishing, playing ball with the boys in the sandlot behind our house (I was *not* an undesirable, last-chosen teammate), or working in the carpenter shop he had set up in the back of the garage.

"Linda, look at this." My dad laid down his hammer and held up the three-cornered shelves he had just finished. "We've got it!"

"I've got mine, too." I pushed toward him an

ocean liner I was crafting, wood scrap upon wood scrap.

"Shall we take it to the lake with us?" he asked.

"When?" I was eager to go. The lake meant fishing, and that was as good as woodworking.

"Next week. Today we've got to finish this, and later we'll play ball."

Saturday after Saturday, while he measured and cut planks lying across sawhorses and created boxes and shelves, I hammered away on leftover pieces of wood and envisioned my projects turning out as well as his. I did little more than make messes and give myself painful blue thumbnails, but my dad never noticed the debris left in my trail. And a sore thumb was a small price to pay for the pleasure of his attention.

I was the son he never had. I became a tomboy, Dale Evans style, with boots, skirt, vest, and a hat that bounced against the back of my shoulders. I took part in battle after neighborhood battle until truces were called when my dad came home for dinner. A few years later, when the cowboy-and-Indian wars evolved into sandlot football scrimmages, I was the player who was most feared—the bully of the block. I remember one angry parent confronting my father: "You'd better control your daughter," he stormed. I had given his son a black eye.

Almost overnight, junior high school revolutionized my outlook. Boys became more than baseball buddies; clothes became more than play costumes; and faces—female faces—deserved applications more delicate than the family bar of soap.

Dad was less than pleased with my new attitudes. The first time I walked out of my parents' room wearing Mom's lipstick, he exploded. "What do you think you're doing?" In his mind I was ruining everything; I had scrubbed the war paint off my face to apply girlish shades of pink make-up. From then on he seemed distant, as if he had suddenly realized that I wasn't a boy.

Mother, however, was delighted by my newly discovered femininity. Years before, she had enrolled me in ballet lessons in an effort to divert my attention from football. At last her prodding and nature's own timing were bearing fruit. Suddenly, I was asking her to buy me skirts instead of overalls and dress shoes instead of sneakers.

"Where were you today?" Dad asked me at dinner one evening. That afternoon had been the first time I had chosen to be with Mom and my sisters instead of with him.

"I wanted to go shopping."

"Shopping?" he asked as if it were some disease. "What's gotten into you? Aren't we buddies anymore?"

"Yes, but shopping is fun. I'm growing up, Daddy."

"So you are," he said sadly, as if he knew he couldn't do anything to stop some impending disaster.

I told him I loved him—but not until the next Father's Day. By then he had grown accustomed to my aloof teenage ways.

Did he love me even though I wasn't at his side?

I never asked. But I hoped so.

Although my interests changed, my energy level did not waver one bit; I still wanted to be a part of whatever was going on. I was always center-stage and not to be outdone by anyone. One afternoon, when I was twelve and old enough to know better, I made a daring proposal to my best friend, Connie, who was at our house enjoying the benefits of Mom's open-door policy—friends were always welcome. My sister Carole, who was in high school, was entertaining her steady boyfriend, Allan, whom she later married. I liked Allan. Being a happy-go-lucky sort, he humored me (what better way to capture my sister's heart?), and that charming quality of his got me into trouble.

"Connie," I said, "I'm going to ask Allan if I can drive his car around the block."

Connie neither egged me on nor tried to dissuade me. She wasn't surprised by anything that came from my cocky head. A ride around the block in Allan's souped-up '54 Ford sounded fun to her.

I ran into the house and made my request to the unsuspecting Allan. "Sure. Here are the keys." He pulled them from his pocket and threw them into my hand.

Whoa! I knew I had managed to get myself into a corner. I hadn't counted on Allan's trust. (He hadn't counted on my nerve.) I could not tolerate retreat. What would Connie think of me? What would Allan think if he knew I didn't even know the meaning of the letters P R N D L above the steering column? Connie and I headed for the driveway and jumped into the front seat of his car.

I put the key in the ignition and started the car. It wouldn't go anywhere in Park. How fortunate that Reverse was the first shifting position. Out of the driveway we rolled. We again went nowhere in Neutral but, once in Drive, we rolled down Duncan Drive toward Twenty-fifth Street. I managed the corner, and the next on Moundview, when a slight curve in the road threw me off course. If I had maneuvered the big turns, why not a little one? But the car came to a stop in a grassy front yard.

Within seconds, Allan and Carole, who had been chasing us, appeared at the car door. Allan, sighing with relief that we—and his car—were safe, moved into the driver's seat and promptly, silently, delivered us home.

I knew what awaited me: a sobering welcome. Dad's arms would be folded across his chest, and his face would be framed with severity.

"Go to your room," he demanded when I walked in the door, "and think about what you've done."

I went to my bedroom and thought. I was crushed that I had provoked him, but I was also satisfied that I had pulled my stunt without causing anyone harm. And I was more than a little heady with my first real taste of independence.

That same year I was introduced to the world of feminine popularity—cheerleader style. Capper Junior High didn't choose its cheering squad by ability alone. No panel of gym teachers or experienced cheerleaders voted for the most qualified. Those of us who were willing to chance defeat in the hope of victory had to try out in front of the most particular judges: the entire student body.

Did I practice! Jumping. Stretching. Splitting. Bending. Smiling. Shouting. Exuding. Although athletics were not new to me, charm was. I no longer played in the back sandlot; I played in front of a mirror.

I awoke with a nervous stomach on the day of the pep rally. All the practice imaginable couldn't take the edge off the real thing. Mom sent me out the door with enthusiastic encouragements, pumping confidence into my spirit. Her daughter would be a winner.

And I was.

When the results were announced, my heart took its first womanly flight. After all, I had not only caught the attention of the crowd in the bleachers, I had broken through the ranks of social prejudice. I was one of only two squad members who didn't live in Westboro, *the* elite section of town where the houses seemed big enough to get lost in and where people were paid to manicure the lawns.

"H'm, I must be made of pretty good stuff," I told myself. I confirmed my opinion in the full-length mirror that reflected a figure that was coming into its own. "I have what it takes." Such sentiments settled into my mind and made themselves as comfortable as a bear in a cave in the winter.

Sometimes I think of my teens as one long pep rally. Not that I was a cheerleader every year—I dropped that official title when I went into high school. My enthusiasm and shouts of "Go! Go! Go!" supported more than a sports team. They supported life—my life and whatever encircled it. Informal get-togethers with friends, sports events, play rehearsals, picnics, swim parties, and double dates filled my days. If I ever found myself alone, I read the latest *Seventeen* magazine while listening to the "top forty" on the radio. Boredom plagued wallflowers—not me. Before I learned to drive, chauffeuring was Mom's nearly full-time occupation.

To guarantee that I would always be in the middle of the social whirlwind, Mom enrolled me in a local charm school. There, women who had sat through similar classes years before passed on their secrets of grace. Was it really a course in acting? Maybe, for they taught the intricate details of perfectly masking one's face, of speaking clearly, of reciting the proper lines at the proper times, of correctly executing entrances and exits, of choosing appropriate costumes, and of walking in four-inch spike heels while never turning an ankle.

I practiced walking with great fervor. With a book balanced on my head, I would start at one end of the hallway and walk to the far wall where my gaze was firmly fixed. My first attempts were slow; then I gradually picked up speed and confidence. My sister Janet, too young to appreciate the importance of such intense striving, laughed at me. Mom, who had replaced Dad as my biggest fan, applauded my successes and lightly dismissed my failures. She knew, and I was learning, which feminine qualities could turn a man's head. Dad watched from afar, secretly proud of my popularity and my "fight," if not of the arena in which I had chosen to do battle.

I missed the camaraderie with Dad, but I was so preoccupied with my teenage concerns that I hardly thought of how I might please him—except by continuing what I was doing: winning at everything I put my mind to.

When I was sixteen, Mom called Janet (my eleven-year-old sister) and me into the family room for a conference. It was important, she said. Although we knew she had been sick recently, we had no inkling of what her announcement would be.

The meeting was short. The instant the word "pregnant" hit my ears, I let out a whoop and ran out of the house. By this time I had learned how to drive (on a stick-shift Volkswagen). I quickly shared Mother's expectations with every friend in the neighborhood. A celebration was in order.

I didn't remember the family trauma, but I knew Mom had miscarried twin boys when I was five years old, before Janet was born. We all hoped this latest pregnancy would end with Mom presenting Dad a healthy, authentic boy, one who would never outgrow the woodshop as I had.

Mom's prolonged ill-health did not prevent us from making a summer trip to the West Coast to visit Carole, who had married Allan and moved to

California. Carole was also expecting. Mom's announcement gave us a double dose of expectation because her delivery was scheduled a few weeks before Carole's. Janet, Mom, and I boarded a cross-country train and headed west.

By nightfall, I wished we had never left home. My hopes for a fun-filled vacation vanished with the sunlight; my stomach ache intensified to the point of being called stomach pains.

"Probably just motion sickness or that greasy hamburger you ate at the drive-in restaurant," Mom assured me. "Get some sleep, and it'll go away."

But it didn't. I felt as if someone were twisting a knife into me. As the train threaded through the mountains of New Mexico, I began to vomit. Mom rang for the conductor.

He took one look at me and announced: "Appendicitis. Seen it lots of times in these mountains. Motion brings it on, you know."

I moaned.

"Better find a doctor," he concluded, and then he vanished.

Within minutes, the train screeched to a halt. The passengers woke from their sleep and leaned out of the doorways of their cabins to see what was causing the unexpected commotion. They watched as I was carried off the train and loaded into a waiting jeep. The makeshift ambulance delivered Mom, Janet, and me to a nearby small-town hospital where a young doctor, fresh out of med school and quite nervous, quickly examined me. I was too sick to care who was poking around.

"Immediate surgery," I heard him pronounce, and then everything went black.

He got what he was looking for—my appendix—but not without leaving his mark. The incision became infected and had to be lanced—

the scar still resembles a chasm cut into a smooth hillside.

After the jittery, embarrassed doctor had repaired his work, Mom announced that Dad was coming to New Mexico to see me.

"Am I *that* sick?"

"No. You're fine. Janet and I will go on to Carole's, and he'll come keep you company."

"But it's so far. What about the office?"

"He *wants* to come."

"He'll drive all that way?" I raised my eyebrows in disbelief.

"What are you complaining about?" Mom was growing slightly testy.

"Who's complaining?" I gave up my questions and welcomed the favor of his company.

For a week he sat by my side and played cards with me. He brought me books. Although small talk was not his forte, he managed to reminisce about his past and talk about his office work.

I loved it, gulping in every word as a hungry lion downs chunks of meat.

Dad and I drove back home together. If any jealousy had been seeping into my mind (*Would this new baby take Dad's attention even further from me?*), it, for a while, evaporated. My dad loved me enough to come to my rescue, to give me a week of his time.

I recommitted myself to making him proud of me. I would be what he had nicknamed me, his "Light" Linda.

When our family was safely tucked into our Topeka nest and I had begun my senior year in high school, Mom gave birth to her fourth daughter, Billie Ann.

Being a typical high-school student, I thought I deserved a little extra financial support. A part-time job at the local dress shop proved the answer to my spending needs. After school and on Saturdays, I helped customers create the look they only vaguely knew they wanted. I helped keep track of inventory and collected money in the cash register. The job ushered me into a world of glamor and flashing lights that captured my smile—and more.

I was a perfect size nine. I didn't lack an inch anywhere. My natural endowments and the skills I had acquired at charm school caught the attention of the store manager. "Linda," she said, "how would you like to model at the store's trunk showings?"

"Wow!" I squealed. "I'd love to." At the showings I unveiled the new season's fashions.

"How about a television commercial?" the manager asked one day.

"I'm game," I said.

Then came modeling sessions at a local photographic studio called Wichers. One print of me wearing a wide-striped bathing suit and sitting precariously on a high, wooden stool was entered by the Wichers' photographer, Dale Williams, in a state photo contest.

Every time I saw Dale he would remind me of the upcoming Miss Topeka Contest. "You've got it in the bag," he would say. "There won't even be any competition. You'll be on your way to Miss Kansas, and then Miss Universe in no time."

When he started talking like that, I just put on a bigger smile and imagined he was right. I asked him more questions. "Why Miss Universe and not Miss America?"

"Timing. The local Miss America Pageant is too far away. We've got to get you in the limelight now."

"Isn't there a step between Miss Kansas and Miss Universe?" Although my view of the world was thoroughly midwestern (*Isn't Manhattan the home of the Kansas State Wildcats?*), I knew the universe included continents and islands too numerous to count.

Dale laughed and explained that contestants from each of the fifty states as well as the larger western countries competed in the relatively new Miss Universe Pageant. In 1962, in other words, Kansas *was* only one step away from the universe.

Dale didn't need to spend time and energy convincing me or Mom that I should enter. The contest could be my ticket to success; it would mean publicity, attention, and formal recognition. It might even win Dad's smile of approval—there would be no more doubt in my mind. The paradox, even then, seemed clear; with the beauty I had acquired and refined, I would work for the wages of his friendship that I had forfeited the day I left the ball field to look at myself in the mirror.

Mother and I loved to shop. During my high-school years, she was particularly generous when it came to buying me the coveted dyed-to-match skirt and sweater sets that were popular with the fashionable crowd at school. We found three at the Grace shop: a dark peach, an avocado, and a powder blue with a sailor collar and tie.

There, Mom and I also discovered an evening gown that promised success: a heavy satiny aqua sheath with boat neck and cap sleeves. It was the little extras that made the dress—stitched accordion pleats down the front, from the shoulders to the waist where a bow rested perfectly.

I knew the bathing suit in which I had posed for Dale Williams was a winner. Mom and I decided to stay with the black, tan, and white stripes, which had propelled me into the pageant in the first place.

I was ready for two of the three judged categories: evening dress and bathing suit. The third—the interview—loomed before me. I had no idea what the roomful of judges would ask. They would want immediate and articulate answers to their questions. Quick thinking and sharp opinions were the indications of having the right stuff.

Which I had.

The first banner draped across my shoulder read "Miss Topeka." The second, "Miss Kansas."

The cheers of the audience, the hugs of my competitors, the lights surrounding the walkway, the flashes of cameras, the fragrance of roses—they all dizzied me.

The best in the state. Wouldn't Dad be proud!

My boyfriend, Ben Hearn,* drove Mom, Margaret (our widowed neighbor), and me to the train station and, like a gentleman, carried our bags to the track marked Miami. Destination: the Miss Universe Pageant.

I drank in his goodby kiss and settled into my window seat. Although nervous and hopeful about the coming week, I had the time to reflect during the two-day trip.

In the months since the Miss Kansas competition, I had grappled with the question that confronts every high-school graduate: What comes next? Serious thoughts about the future had never more than flitted through my head, and therefore an empty September had caught me by surprise. What *was* next?

The monotonous clickety-clack of the train prompted more reflection. Although I hadn't been a student who was preoccupied with studies, I was used to spending my days in a classroom. College, I had thought, might be an interesting extension of my routine, and the local Washburn University provided easy access to a familiar environment of

*Not his real name.

old friends. It couldn't hurt to give it a try. Enrolling as an undecided major, I registered for fifteen hours of general freshman courses and moved my closet of clothes from my room in my parents' house to the sorority house where I had been quickly admitted.

The only interesting things about college were the men and the social life. One man, in particular, caught my eye.

The "10" of the Phi Delta Theta fraternity, Ben Hearn, was the talk of every sorority house. His dark hair, Rock Hudson frame, and smile, so warm it could melt winter into summer, were legendary. I knew who he was even before he introduced himself and drew me into conversation over a lunchtime card game in the student union. Before long he was a regular at our ten-point pitch table and a regular Friday-night date.

I took Ben home to meet my family (meaning Dad). Mom outdid herself. She single-handedly created a roast-beef dinner and served it on her rarely seen, best china. Twelve-year-old Janet and baby Billie were perfectly mannered. Although I had always been surrounded by men, the ones I formally brought home to dinner could be counted on one's thumbs.

The son of a lawyer, Ben was taking prelaw courses. His credentials were as impressive as his appearance. I was counting on Dad, who had recently given up his successful real-estate business to join the management of a large savings-and-loan corporation, to approve of my catch. By the time we all had swallowed our last bites of German apple cake, Dad's eyes were smiling with approval. Ben had passed the test; Dad thought I had found a good one.

When at last the train's conductor called "Miami," we walked down the steep steps to the welcome of the bright, hot sun. Miami was more than I had dreamed it would be. I had never seen such sites nor stayed in such a luxurious hotel. I had never even seen the ocean—either ocean. Standing on the beach between the pulsating water held in a bowl bigger than all fifty states, and the city skyline, a host of the high life and glamor I had previously glimpsed only in magazine stills, I sensed I wanted to see more. *What else have I been missing in Topeka? If I win the pageant, I will see the world; if not, I will see (I have no idea how or when) the country—east to west.* The comparatively quiet life of a small midwestern city paled in the light of the sun's reflection on the water and at the thought of a star's reflection in a mirror.

The pageant began with the Parade of States, in which each contestant dressed in a costume representative of her culture. Dressed as a sunflower, I paraded down the elevated walkway that was as long as an airport runway. My long-sleeved, tan, itchy leotard flaunted two large chenille-covered sunflowers, one on my left shoulder and one on the right side of my waist.

I blotted from my mind and sight the thousands of eyes that watched me, head to toe, as I put one foot in front of the other. Despite the distracting lights and popping flash bulbs, I concentrated on smiling and walking as if a book were balanced on top of my head.

The second round of judging proceeded much like the first. The twenty contestants who survived the first cuts changed into evening attire, and then we paraded in front of an enthusiastic audience. Feeling comfortable in my tried-and-true aqua gown, I relaxed a little and enjoyed this parade more than the first. *If life could be one long march of beauty,* I thought, *I could live forever on the applause I'm soaking up.*

But at the same time I was dreading the upcoming contest, the interview. I didn't even want to think about it. What if my voice cracked or my mind went blank? When my name was not listed among the twelve semifinalists who were called to interview, I actually sighed with relief.

Even though I wasn't Miss Universe, my bid had been a success. I had been introduced to a new world. For a week I had enjoyed the company of the most beautiful women in the world. (I was one of them!) We had partied, dined, laughed, and made memories that would last a lifetime.

Mom was more disappointed in my runner-up status than I was. Her soaring hopes plummeted, and when she greeted me after the announcement of the cut, her eyes brimmed with tears.

"It's okay, Mom!" I light-heartedly consoled her, the smile still covering my face.

It seemed odd for me to be comforting her, as if she, not I, had been judged less than the world's number one.

What was a title anyway? If I were close enough to perfection to march with the best, I was close enough to hold my head high and return home—a winner.

2 Fast Flight Nowhere

Now Kansas *was* a black-and-white movie.

I had seen a corner of the Land of Oz and wanted to see every square mile of it.

Nothing had ever seemed as boring to me as college did—the lectures that droned on and on, the hours I reluctantly spent reading textbooks and writing papers, the point of which I didn't understand. Ben and the parties we attended were school's salvation, but I could keep up my social schedule only if I let go of the academics. Dropping out of school wouldn't make me less in demand on weekends.

Late in December of my third semester, I decided that school and I were a bad mix. I had already made up my mind to quit when I told my friend and sorority sister, Susan, of my plans. Susan was a level-headed kind who had some concept of life after Saturday night. She did her best to dissuade me. "You can't just walk into the registrar's office and say you're not going to take your exams."

"I most certainly can," I retorted in a firm, decisive manner, characteristic of my not-so-practical mindset.

"You're so close to the end. Even if you don't study you could get Cs and have something to show for your semester. If you leave now, you'll get fifteen hours of straight F. Someday you'll regret it."

Nothing she said affected me. I wanted what I wanted—out, and I didn't care that it meant quitting the week before exams. But I dreaded telling Dad. I dreaded telling him so much that I told him only that I was not going to go back the following semester.

Having worked himself up the local ladder of success without the benefit of a college degree, Dad clearly enumerated to me the benefits of seeing the year through. His most impressive argument was that a college education looked good on anybody's record.

"It's boring, Dad, and I've got all the record I'll ever need—this." I stood on my steady, shapely legs and posed as only a trained model can. I stopped talking long enough for an imaginary camera to click my closed-mouth smile and then rejoiced in my victory.

I was no longer a kid who had to take orders. A scowling "Go to your room" wouldn't make a twenty-year-old arrogant beauty queen turn her back and march off. I dropped out of school, but to smooth things over a little, I left the house every day during final week. *My secret,* I thought. *What he doesn't know, won't hurt him.* I was thankful that he never asked to see my grades.

Dad's final remark on the matter of my quitting school—"If that's what you want"—ushered me into adulthood, exactly where I thought I belonged.

Shortly after I left school, my sister Carole came for a visit. The whole time she was home, she tried to convince me to return with her to California for a short time. "No excuses; I'll pay your air fare."

"But you know I'm afraid to fly—that's why we took a train to Miami."

"Lin-*da*," she said somewhat impatiently, "being afraid of something you've never tried doesn't make any sense. I'm buying your tickets. I need a break from washing diapers and cleaning. I want you to see Southern California."

Carole had a way of always saying the right thing. I had never seen her home, and I would not be shamed by being afraid of something as commonplace as flying.

I went—and that, my first flight, was the last one I boarded not knowing the model of the aircraft. Only the first five minutes frightened me, and excitement as much as fear caused my stomach to churn. As the plains, the Rockies, and the desert slid under my feet, I watched hostesses, not as pretty as myself, servicing the galley, working their way across the country I so much wanted to see.

I had discovered my sightseeing ticket!

When I returned home, I filled out an application with TWA, whose central headquarters were in Kansas City. It wasn't long before I was called for an interview. On the appointed day Ben and I drove eastward an hour to 10 Richards Road, Kansas City, Missouri. Ben amused himself at the nearby airport while I found my way to a large room filled with hopeful applicants. When I entered, I quickly glanced at the heads of the seated young women. I wanted to see how many would be automatically disqualified for walking in hatless and gloveless. Having been tipped off, I confidently sported my perfect attire. As if we had come for a doctor's appointment, we were called one at a time and directed down a nondescript hallway through an office doorway. The woman who greeted us, or at least me, looked like a stewardess who had reached the maximum age allowed for active TWA duty and been retired to a desk job.

She asked me a long series of "What would you do if . . ." questions pertaining to emergency situations and then sent me on to a second, male interviewer who fired a battery of seemingly pointless questions. Several written aptitude tests followed, and, although the appointment ended with the standard "Don't call us, we'll call you" farewell, the female interviewer slipped me a pleasant "We'll see you soon."

I returned her smile; that was exactly what I had expected I would hear.

Within a week I received a telegram. I was "in" and to report immediately to Kansas City for eight weeks of flight school.

In 1963 only the *crème de la crème* were deemed worthy of serving airline passengers. Buying a plane ticket bought a traveler the privilege of watching a single, pretty, not-too-short, tall, fat, or thin, perfectly groomed and mannered young woman walk up and down the galley, smiling and pleasantly chatting all the way. Only three out of forty applicants opened affirming telegrams. We welcomed them as avidly as some people might open an invitation to an exclusive party or a letter of acceptance to Harvard.

I moved into the school "dormitory," an apartment-hotel on Kansas City's luxurious Plaza. From there, my three roommates and I rode back and forth to the training center by cab in the morning and bus in the evening. This kind of schooling I could hack. Although the all-day class schedule was rigorous and the instructors, who gave weekly exams, demanding, I knew exactly why I was there and what rewards lay at the far end of the course: *adventure.*

Before we were even taken inside a real aircraft, we had memorized, from full-sized mockups, the ins and outs, nooks and crannies of ten different props and jets, on which we might work. We had analyzed case study after case study of typical passenger behavior, establishing acceptable and expected hostess reactions to any person's inquiries, apprehensions, or needs. We had learned the dress code and the TWA good-grooming formula, which included the regulation shade of lipstick and nail polish that would be periodically checked by the supervisors.

I sat through these long classes never questioning the rigidity of the demands made on us. The uniformity of our dress, down to the stipulation that we all change from winter wear to summer wear on a specified day, that we change from our "spikes" to our lower-heeled work shoes first thing after every take-off, and that we never board or leave a plane without wearing gloves, hat, and dress shoes seemed reasonable. Much like the military, we were a special and honored group. Our uniforms and the care with which we wore them symbolized, to ourselves and to the airline's customers, perfection.

By the end of the eight-week training course, the instructors had succeeded in convincing us of our status: we were the chosen few.

Along with the eleven other members of my TWA class, I spent the first six months of my employment waiting for the phone to ring. Rookies provided the company with an ever-ready and eager second string, always on reserve, in case a scheduled hostess was sick. When your name reached the top of the reserve list (anytime, night or day), you were called (TWA always had a number where you could be reached) and given

Fast Flight Nowhere

33

three hours to report for work, one hour before take-off.

Wanting to be near Ben and the now-familiar party life of his frat house, I listed Kansas City as my first-choice domicile. Chicago, being reasonably close and relatively exciting, came up second, and Los Angeles, Carole's home, third.

Kansas City was agreeable with some faceless person in the placement department, so I settled into a five-room furnished apartment, which I shared with three co-workers, one of them my childhood friend, Connie.

I was on my own. The adult version of the good life had begun. The day finally came when I could join the ranks of the scheduled and bid for flights. The day finally dawned when, proudly if not expectantly, I walked into room 100 of the 10 Richards Road headquarters and filled out my first bid sheet, a piece of 8 ½ by 11 paper covered with numbers, which when decoded, named cities, counted meals or snacks served, and enumerated hours in flight and on the ground. In this world, seniority counted for everything. My friend Ginger and I requested the most exotic flights on the sheet with layovers in Los Angeles and New York, knowing full well we would be assigned the bottom of the line prop job, flight 326. For months we saw no action more exciting than one commuter flight that lit down in St. Louis, Indianapolis, Terre Haute, Dayton, Cincinnati, then reversed itself, all the way back to Kansas City— four times a week.

But Ginger and I made the best of that run, which most hostesses despised. On Valentine's Day and then again on Easter we decorated the plane's interior with seasonal color. In Dayton, the layover city, we frequently partied with the crew.

One of these early flights brought a halt to my rather naïve view of my womanly powers of which no one had ever taken advantage. The lengthy and tiring trip was almost over. We were on the last leg of the up-and-down flight when I went to the rear of the plane to check on our only passenger. Although we could not serve a person more than two drinks per "service," there was no reasonable limit to the amount of alcohol one could buy and consume from the beginning to the end of a puddle-jumper flight such as 326, on which we served four separate meals or snacks. Ginger and I had paid no attention to this businessman's frame of mind, and eager to be hospitable, I offered him coffee, a pillow, and a blanket.

"No. No," he answered. "I'm quite comfortable. But it's lonely back here, why don't you join me?"

He offered me the seat next to his, by the window. As I settled in for a chat about the current midwestern economy and life in his home town, he turned on the overhead reading lamp, placing me in the spotlight of the otherwise dark cabin. He obviously approved of the sight, and behind my professional smile, I approved of his attention, until he suddenly lunged on top of me, pinning me flat on my back, as the latch that should have held the seat upright snapped. We were thrust into the "reclining" position.

Normally, our orders decreed that we were *never* to make a scene. Unless a passenger was unruly, he or she was always right. If anyone caused us real trouble we were to push a buzzer in the back of the plane to signal one of the crew to appear from behind the cabin door. But how could I push a button I couldn't reach since I was held captive by a man I couldn't budge. An audience would have prevented my predicament, and being acutely aware of the row upon row of empty seats, I felt no qualms about letting out a scream that immediately attracted Ginger's attention.

Within seconds, the flight engineer stood over

the lonely businessman who received a royal tongue-lashing. I locked myself in the rest room and cried. I had been physically restrained for less than thirty seconds, but I had nearly drowned in the feelings of helplessness and vulnerability that had flooded my head.

I breathed in deeply, a reminder to myself that I was fine—healthy and free—but it was nearly a month before I could walk toward the back of a plane and feel no fear of being caught with no place to run.

Every time I tore a page off my month-by-month calendar, I came closer to my dream: working the enviable flights. Eventually I saw the country—Los Angeles, San Francisco, Las Vegas, Phoenix, New York, Boston, Washington, D.C., Philadelphia, Chicago. With other crew members or alone I took in the sights and sounds of each city. In Indianapolis and Terre Haute I had spent empty hours watching the radar screen or reading romance novels, but not anymore. Each month I bid for a different flight and each month I tackled one or more new cities. The minute the passengers had deplaned and I was free to leave, I headed for the action. What are now called "singles' bars" were, as much as the hotels in which I was booked, my layover "home." Men? I found them—or they found me. I could outdance them all, but I knew just how to leave at exactly the right moment, always leaving them hungry for what they wanted but didn't get.

It was a game; when you're at the top, you get to lay down the rules.

But one morning I woke up in Los Angeles, particularly puzzled that in the preceding weeks I had tackled more than cities. For no reason I would lose my balance, then catch myself. I could hardly believe I had actually walked into the bulkhead. The first time, I convinced myself, the plane had jerked, much like one convinces oneself that a mouse did *not* just dive behind the refrigerator when it most certainly did. But the second, third, and fourth times reinforced reality. I knew that some absent-minded or clumsy people frequently bruise themselves from misjudging distances or not noticing their surroundings, but not I. I had spent too many hours learning how to control my every move. *What was happening? Was I losing my touch? Why was I, the life of the party, now inventing excuses to stay in and go to bed early?* There was no room in my mind for such reflections. They tried to set up camp in my consciousness, but I repeatedly pulled out their stakes. I would just be more watchful and careful of my movements on the plane.

But the day before this particular morning, on the relatively short flight from Las Vegas to Los Angeles, I had slipped—and been found out. A piece of strawberry chiffon pie had slid off a serving tray in my hand and plunged down the front of a middle-aged man in a gray flannel suit. The pink gel skimmed his shirt and tie. What didn't stick there settled onto his lap. Both he and I gasped in disbelief; my very first breath exhaled an "I'm sorry" so intense it softened the passenger like putty in my hands. As soon as he realized what had happened, he started absolving me: "It's all right . . ."

"No. No. Let me help you. I don't know what happened. . . . Here, a towel."

"No. It's *all* right. . . . It'll come out. I have another suit with me."

"We'll pay for the cleaning, of course—"

Our conversation proceeded along similar lines until he was as comfortable as possible, considering the circumstances, and I had exhausted my reserve of apologies.

He may have forgiven me, but forgiving myself was quite a different matter.

The pie spill triggered a stabbing, secret fear. *If it had happened once, it could surely happen again.* The next passenger might not be so pleasant and neither might my supervisor if word reached her. TWA hostesses did not make a practice of filling people's laps with food.

I had always believed that fear had a way of slowly draining a person's energy. But my energy level, which had once been like a fountain, full and overflowing, disappeared as rapidly as if a giant sewer pipe were at the base of that fountain.

My schedule, which had once called for flying all day and dancing all evening, now included an occasional two-day-long sleep.

Serving one meal to a planeload of passengers left me tired enough to wish I could head straight for the couch in the crew lounge when we landed. Could I keep up this pace forever? Especially without letting anyone know that I was anything less than my old light-hearted self? The question persistently hammered at my consciousness, like an unwelcome visitor at the door. Ignoring it did not make it go away. In the middle of the night it haunted me. Was *this* a secret I could keep?

Ben, who for two years had been a frequent and favored date, had repeatedly asked me to marry him. I had repeatedly put him off, saying I wasn't ready to settle down. I would be content to keep house and have children when I was ready—too old to welcome passengers on board a flying machine.

But I proved an easy pushover when he punctuated his words with a diamond ring. It promised a slower-paced life, a chance to get rested up before I would plunge into the more established next step—mortgaged ranch houses, country-club entertaining, and children on my lap.

On a cold January weekend in 1965 I went home to Topeka to make our engagement official. Dad quickly approved of our homemaking plans and celebrated my success at finding a perfect husband by giving us a dinner at the country club. In one handsome man I had found my emergency exit from a hectic life and the fulfillment, although ahead of my original schedule, of my—of any girl's—dream—a march down the happily-ever-after aisle.

Dad captured the spirit of the evening with the family movie camera. I threw my arms around Ben's neck, flashing my diamond in front of the blinding flood lights. I belonged to the best catch in Kansas.

In June, two months after I, only slightly nostalgic for the airborne life, quit my TWA job, we married—in a Cinderella wedding ceremony that provided the ladies of the city with weeks' worth of conversation.

The day lacked nothing but the anointing of God.

When I look back on my first marriage, I think of Shakespeare's commentary on life:

All the world's a stage,
And all the men and women merely players:
They have their exits and their entrances.

If I had only known then what I know now—the meaning of love, God's love, Christian love—things would have been so much different. I could have been concerned for something other than myself and the way I had to be in control by guarding each movement.

Ben and I shared a bed, laughed with each

other, ate together, socialized as a couple as if we were plastic figures in a child's dollhouse or actors in a movie. In a way, marriage was a subdued, prolonged, and private version of a cocktail party—pleasant, though insignificant and soon-forgotten, chitchat.

What was behind his Rock Hudson façade? I didn't know. Nor did he know what was behind my cover-girl smile.

Dad got him a respectable savings-and-loan job in Midland, Texas, and there we settled into a furnished apartment. I unwrapped our carful of wedding gifts, followed cookbook instructions (I *did* know how to boil an egg), arranged and rearranged knickknacks on shelves I shined, and grew bored with small-town living. Ben went off to an office and spent nine hours a day doing heaven knows what. He never offered to explain what he did. I didn't ask.

To combat the boredom, I took a receptionist job at a local oil company. To combat the sluggishness, I went to bed early, talked Ben into our eating a lot of meals out, and began to let the housework slip.

The slower pace of marriage was not significantly improving my health. I was not pregnant, yet I frequently threw up my breakfast. As I once had feared the TWA supervisor would discover my clumsiness, I now feared Ben would discover me vomiting into the Tupperware container I carried in my purse. That and a closetful of other maladies were *my* secret—even after I blacked out at work and hit my head on the corner of my desk.

"I don't find any major problems, Linda." The emergency-room doctor talked straight to me, even though Ben was, by now, at my side.

"Brides often have a hard time adjusting to life

after the wedding reception. We call it 'newlywed jitters,' and it often takes a while to get on an even keel. Take it easy. Get as much rest as you need. Maybe quit your job until you feel better—which you will. It just takes a little time."

It will go away, he had said. And I hung onto his words as if they were a life raft in the midst of a churning river.

One morning I awoke, sweaty and agitated with worry. *It's Sunday,* I thought. *Sunday. Some people go to church. They say it helps them. I wonder what they find.*

"Ben, wake up." I touched his arm to make sure he heard me. "I want to go to church."

"Church?" he groaned.

He had been inside a church about as many times as I had, enough to know the general layout but nothing else.

"Yes. I need to go."

"Whatever for?"

"I don't know. But we must."

"Some other day."

Something inside me was pleading for help, and I stuck to my desire with a will power I rarely showed anymore.

Sensing I wasn't to be silenced, he let me drag him to Midland's most fashionable church.

There, I took in the sights without hearing any comforting words. *God, are you there?* I prayed. Then I waited as if the robed pastor were to respond verbally to my silent question.

I rode home, thinking I should have listened to Ben; I didn't give God another thought for several years.

I quit my job and started spending my days as well as my nights in bed.

My secrets started leaking in spite of my cover-up efforts. Ben would come home from work, and I would still be in my nightgown. "How's it going?" he would ask, and I would burst into tears. "I'll get us something to eat," he would say, eager to get things under control.

"Get yourself something; I don't think I'll eat. I'll sit and watch you," I would answer, but even that response became less and less frequent.

"Linda, I want to help you." At last Ben had cooked enough dinners for himself. "What will make you better?"

I didn't know the answer to his question, but Ben was desperate enough to call my mom. She arrived on the next plane, Billie Ann in hand.

Smiling Mom cooked, cleaned, read to me, tried to coax me into embroidering, sat Billie on my bed, and made her laugh, all while I lay there, not caring whether I lived to see the next sunrise.

After a week, she campaigned for us to move back to Kansas: "A young wife needs the support of her family and her old friends. And who can be anything but depressed in a town paved with red clay and lined with oil refineries?" She addressed her comments to anyone who would listen.

She easily convinced me, and Ben conceded. "If it's what you want," he said and put Mom, Billie, and me on a plane to Topeka and followed, in a few days, with a carload of barely used household goods.

But the sun of Mom's backyard had no magic powers. Nothing roused me from my prone position. She and Ben finally demanded I see another doctor.

The quiet, calculating neurologist at the Menninger Clinic gave me a quick battery of tests. With a hammer he hit my knee and the inside of my elbow, and both times nothing happened. He shined a bright light in my eyes and didn't tell me what he saw.

"Can you touch your finger to your nose?"

I hadn't tried it in a long time, but I knew I could. Everybody could.

Except me.

The room was eerily silent, and then he made his last request: "Why don't you get down and try walking from the table over to the door."

The room was small but the door was at the other end, probably eight feet away. I concentrated my sight on the closed door, imagined a book on top of my head, and put one foot in front of the other again and again until I had maneuvered the distance. I turned around, flushed with embarrassment. I had wavered like a drunk person, which meant I had failed the test, the consequences of which I didn't then grasp.

Even in his prognosis the neurologist said little but referred me to a psychiatrist on staff at the state hospital.

Later in the week, Ben, Mom, and I sought his advice. We sat in the overstuffed waiting-room chairs until I suspected the receptionist thought we were pieces of furniture.

I didn't read any magazines, and I talked to neither Ben nor Mom, who flipped glossy pages faster than they could possibly read them. I knew I needed help, but the months of hiding behind a "there's nothing wrong" mask had taken their toll; I trusted no one more than myself. Mother and Ben were obviously ganging up against me, I whimpered inwardly, and trying to gain power over me—and here I was, too sick to defend myself.

In the examining room I identified various ink blots as objects and associated various words with the thoughts they crystallized. When the last question had been asked, the doctor walked out of the room, leaving me alone to stare at the diplomas on the wall and then at the floor. I prayed to no one for deliverance from myself or the descent I seemed to be making into hell.

After an eternity of lonely silence, Ben, followed by the doctor, came through the doorway. Ben's countenance said nothing new. It had been exclaiming the same worry and confusion for weeks. I didn't like to look at his face; it was too vivid a reminder of what had become of me. I had let him down. I hadn't hosted any gala dinners. I had made him give up a promising job. I was too tired to care that I had been a bad wife—except when I looked into his eyes.

As if I hadn't been in the room, the doctor told Ben where I belonged and when: in the state hospital that very day.

Wonderful, I sighed, relieved that the hell would end, oblivious to the implications of my sentencing. I only knew that, at last, professionals, who knew exactly what they were doing, would take care of me and get me back on my feet. At last I could quit fighting, quit hiding, and, in the haven of a hospital, sleep until they found the prescription that would return my feet to the dance floor.

I felt *sure* my deliverance was at hand.

I crawled through the back door of our new blue Chevrolet (a wedding present from Ben's parents) and lay on my side across the width of the seat. I slid my hands under my cheek and soaked in the familiar womblike comfort of a warm, enclosed moving car.

Ben drove into the hospital's long driveway and slowed to a stop in front of a brick building set on sprawling grounds, spotted with huge spreading shade trees.

I did not ask Ben or Mom for help, yet each took one of my arms and held some of my weight as I climbed the long flight of stone steps they knew I could not manage alone. Mother cooed instructions and encouragements, such as "It'll be all right, honey," into my ear until the thick glass door that kept the fresh windblown sunshine from contaminating the musty inside air swung shut behind us.

3 *Why Have You Forsaken Me?*

As a library checkout separates borrowers from lenders, a formidable admittance desk separated us from the stocky middle-aged nurse behind it. She had been expecting us and recited how one went about making this hospice a home. There was a ream of forms to be filled out. Again, Mom and Ben took over. For half an hour they sketched out my life's history. Only occasionally, as I leaned like an extension ladder against the massive desk, did they ask me for facts they had forgotten or never known.

"Ben, please hurry," I mumbled. "Mom, can't you write any faster? Just see me to a bed, and let Ben fill out the forms." But the nurse clearly was in charge and had no intention of letting me leave the high-ceilinged room until she had gathered all the needed information.

Finally, she nodded in our direction, and two orderlies immediately marched toward me.

"We'll take you to your ward, Linda," one said.

I winced at hearing the word "ward," but took

Ben's arm, eager to follow the white-suited college students to a resting place.

In that instant, the orderly caught Ben's eye, then deliberately focused his stare on the glass doors we had just entered. He may as well have barked a command: "Take her mother and leave—now." Ben and Mom obeyed like foot soldiers.

"They'll find the problem, Linda," mother assured as she walked backward toward the front entrance.

"It's what the doctor ordered," Ben reminded me, affectionately touching Mom's shoulder.

"What are you *doing?*" I gasped. I suddenly trusted *only* my family and wanted them at my side. "You've got to see where I'm staying. You can't *leave* me here."

"Linda. . . ." Mother looked as if she were drowning, but she, or rather I, was at the mercy of two orderlies who each took one of my arms.

"We'll be back soon," Mom assured as if she were telling herself as much as me that I was not being taken away. Ben led her outside.

The touch of the orderlies' hands stirred up the old fight in me. Being deserted was horror enough for one day; I would not also be humiliated by being dragged by strangers. With all the control I could muster, I set my jaw and firmly declared, "I can do it myself."

They released their grip and I, not about to make a scene, stepped toward the women's ward.

Walk. I had never sent such a determined command to my legs, and never had they so firmly refused to budge. In the course of five steps the muscles rebelled like the Prodigal Son. One of them would not support my weight while the other moved from the rear to the forward position.

I stood still and felt my pride, my identity, seep

away. Not that I wanted to let it escape; I had no choice. I had two options and neither would allow me any self-respect: I could ask for help, or I could stumble across the floor. The moment demanded a quick evaporation of the Linda who had always been able to take care of herself.

With tears in my eyes I whispered, "Can you help?" and the young men gently resumed their roles as human canes.

I now thank God that He, in His mercy, veils the future from us, for I could not have handled knowing I would never again walk without aid.

We took the visitor's route to a new wing of the complex. We turned a corner onto Rappaport North. The cafeteria and a pleasantly furnished lounge where patients could chat with friends and family caught my eye. For a hospital, it was homey enough to set me slightly at ease. But . . .

Then I saw beyond the camouflage. A long, high, full-to-overflowing planter had tempered the severity of the heavy steel door that separated the lounge from the ward, and it hid from view the dangling padlock.

As one of the orderlies turned a key and popped the latch, I asked, "Is that lock to keep people out or in?"

His reply was vague: "It's for the protection of the patients."

The meaning of *state hospital* suddenly penetrated my skull. The people behind that door were not sick; they were crazy! And I had been relegated to their ranks. What was I supposed to have seen in those ink blots? Was my life going to be in danger? Would I have to listen to people telling me they were Napoleon—or Jesus?

State hospital. Surely it was the name of another planet, and surely I didn't belong in outer space.

The nurses who greeted me needed more information to fill more folders for my file. At their glassed-in station they wrote down my answers to their questions; I wondered if any of them believed what I was saying or if they thought I was making it up as I went along. But more than anything I wanted to go to bed and sleep off this bad dream.

In time, one of the nurses showed me to my room, escorting me to the quarter that was mine. "Linda, this is your locker, your night stand, and your bed."

Just what I had been waiting for. I grabbed the top of the bedsheet, pulled it down, and started to climb in.

The nurse firmly reprimanded me: "Linda, we don't go to bed around here until nine o'clock."

Since when was someone telling me that I could or could not nap?

"But—"

"No 'buts.' Rules are rules, and you'll have to stay up until bedtime."

I quickly learned other strictly enforced regulations as well. Everyone had an assigned daily job. Mine was clearly explained. At the sink in the corner of the ward's television room, I was to wash the medicine cart. Given no choice, I listened to the instructions and then sat down to pass the hours until bedtime in front of the television, making only mild attempts to make acquaintance with the roomful of strangers who acted more subdued than crazy.

After dinner I had an urge to put my life in order: *I'll bathe. Shave my legs. Get myself looking presentable. Then I'll be able to face tomorrow.* Such a plan was so much a part of me that it was nearly subconscious, but it always put me to bed thinking I would wake up feeling better. Tomorrow would make me well.

I had not brought a razor with me; if I had, it would have been taken from me. The regulations allowed for only limited use of such articles. "We have razors here at the desk that may be signed out for short periods of time," explained the evening nurse who said she would help me with my bath.

I wanted to snap "yes, sir" and salute, but I took her arm instead and plodded past my room to the rest rooms at the far end of the women's wing. The nurse stayed close-by, but we agreed that I would take care of my personal needs as much as possible.

Once in the tub I proceeded to nip the stubble from my calf. *This used to be such an easy task,* I thought, noticing that the upward strokes were only half cleaning the surface.

"Are you sure you can manage?" she asked from the other side of the closed curtain.

"Everything's fine," I assured her—and myself.

And then I saw the blood.

"I can't do anything right!" I exploded. Tears of anger, frustration, and exhaustion covered my cheeks. The nurse appeared at my side, mended the gash, which still scars my shin, finished the job herself, and put me to bed.

Within a few days the staff psychiatrist gave me a name for my problem: hysterical paralysis.

"Linda, we've got to get to the root of what's bothering you. You're carrying around some deep-seated, unresolved conflict that's overloading and short-circuiting your system. Buried emotions often try to make their escapes through physical upheavals. You've been exhausted, and now you've lost your coordination because you've pent up too much anxiety."

Whatever you say. You're the doctor.

"We'll start with your childhood. . . ."

In typical psychiatric fashion, he dissected my life. It felt as if he were digging holes in my brain, trying to open escape routes through which demons might flee.

But he heard no heart-rending tales, and my debilitation only accelerated to the point where the staff changed my work assignment and declared the cafeteria off limits to me. I could no longer wheel the medicine cart without falling onto the tiled—not carpeted—floor. "We'd like you to sit and fold the laundered linens," the nurse said when she stripped me of my former task. And as to the cafeteria, my trips there too often ended with my fainting. With a few other closely guarded women, I ate my meals in a room adjoining the nurses' station. But within a month of my admittance, I could not tolerate even that strain without blacking out.

The psychiatrist and social workers took delight in tracking my fainting patterns. The when and why of my collapsing was fodder for their analyses. Ben was allowed to visit infrequently, but when he did I invariably fainted. Those tuned-out moments always prompted the staff to probe into the secrets of our marriage.

The doctor, dressed in street clothes, would look me in the eye and, in a hundred different ways, repeat one basic question: "Do you love your husband?"

In one sentence I revealed my ignorance of and apathy toward the subject that seemed to preoccupy him: "What is love?" was all I could answer.

My marriage, good or bad, didn't seem worth the effort Dr. Martinas* was putting into it. It didn't seem worth the effort of words. There was nothing to dig up, nothing on which to base an in-depth, fact-finding conversation. Nothing I said or

*Not his real name.

didn't say seemed to convince the doctor that I was not hysterical—until several months after the night I went to bed and couldn't get up in the morning.

Those sleepy days that grew into weeks and months are a tiny dark speck on my memory. The i.v. bottle dripped life into my veins as I lay in a fetal position, too sick to think about what the rest of the world was doing. One day blurred into the next, making few distinguishable from any of the others. My perfect size-nine figure had previously lost some of its glory, but now my skin was shrunken around my bones; my five-feet-six-inch body shriveled to eighty-five pounds.

During my confinement Dr. Martinas continued his every-other-day consultation. In the course of one bedside visit, he named the cork that when pulled, he thought, would drain away my paralysis. "We've looked over your case carefully and feel that if you divorce your husband, just put that part of your life behind you, we'll have you on your feet."

Hope stuck its head out of the ground: "I *just* want to be well."

"We think this will do the trick."

I'll trade anything to walk, I thought, still hanging on to my faith in medicine, despite any evidence that it was on the right track. If the doctors didn't know what they were doing, who did? My family had given up and asked the professionals for help; there was no where else to go, no one else to trust.

I acquiesced. "Whatever you think is best," and without a thought of anything but my own misery, I agreed to let Ben be cut from my life.

Shortly thereafter, he was called for active Army duty in Vietnam. I never saw him again.

Why isn't it working? I cried in my restless sleep. If I had known how to pray, I would have stormed heaven with intense demands for health. Release from marriage had not affected my condition in the least. *Why don't they try something else? They're not going to let me lie here forever are they?* Questions sped through my mind.

Finally, the doctors questioned their own diagnosis. "Linda, we want to make sure your problem isn't physical. We're going to get you out of bed and give you some tests, get you to physical therapy and into an exercise routine. Maybe you really can do more than you think you can."

The doctor named several tests, including a painful spinal tap. While I was conscious, a neurologist suctioned spinal fluid from my back, at the waist, and then I waited for I had no idea what.

The next day a nurse summoned me to the conference room for what looked like a big powwow. She wheeled me into a room with a long table, around which sat nearly every doctor and nurse on the day staff. All their eyes seemed glued to the table. Some were ashen as if they had just heard of some horror-filled world disaster.

I was seated at the end of the table. Dr. Martinas broke the silence: "We have the results of yesterday's test, and we wanted to share them with everyone."

Despite the pain on the roomful of faces, I brightened. *If they called a meeting, they have found something. If they can give it a new name, they can apply new treatments.*

"There *is* a physical cause for your weakness: multiple sclerosis, a deterioration of your body's nerve endings."

I turned the words *multiple sclerosis* over in my mind as a baby handles a new stuffed animal, examining it from every angle. I had never heard of the disease before, but it sounded manageable.

"Here are some pamphlets," the doctor continued. "I'm sure they'll answer all your questions, and if not, any of the nurses will."

At last! They are admitting I wasn't imagining all this. Finally! They will give me medicines that will make it all go away.

The meeting was quickly over, and I was wheeled to my room where I sat, Indian style, on the center of my bed. As a school girl surrounds herself with paper dolls, I encircled myself with the booklets. They reminded me of the "now you're a woman" pamphlets nervous mothers give adolescent daughters. I quickly saw the "what you can expect" explanations scattered around me were of an adult variety and not terribly specific: "MS symptoms usually appear between the ages of twenty and forty . . . unknown origin . . . abnormal reflect response . . . nerves become scarred . . . messages blocked from brain to muscles . . . gradual deterioration . . . no known cure."

No nurse watched over my reading. The words on the pages administered a torturous death to my hope. I rushed through the first stage of grief—denial. Then the reality of disability settled on me like fog. Hope was washed away by the tears that gushed from my eyes. My year-long assumption—"If they can name it, they can heal it"—had been wrong. For once, identifying the problem was *not* half of the solution. Naming the enemy only poured my helplessness in concrete.

For four months the staff, and particularly one red-haired student nurse, Peggy, worked on me, getting me ready for life in the outside world. Either the long rest in bed or passing through the initial stages of MS had put a stop to my fainting spells. But my muscles had withered with disuse; my mind had grown dull. My new schedule included long hours in the gym where I stretched and was stretched back into some semblance of shape. I tugged on muscles I had never known existed and shouted demands to them that they only half heard and understood. I walked, supporting myself between parallel bars. I grasped arm pulleys, rode an exercise bicycle, and did leg-lifts. But firmer muscles still left me miles away from normal living. *What am I going to do? I can't walk,* haunted all of my thoughts.

I dreaded life outside the safety of the hospital. With the exception of Peggy, I hadn't made any friends here. But I had grown accustomed to these people, the overworked staff and the sedated patients. They didn't ask embarrassing questions. They didn't know I had once been beautiful. They didn't expect me to achieve any success greater than making it through another day. They expected so little of me. Despite my inability to shuffle a deck of cards without it exploding into the air, they enjoyed playing cards with me. I could just imagine my dad sitting at a table, waiting for me to haltingly take my turn. He would sigh. Impatiently fuss. Possibly leave the game, never again to offer himself as a member of the party. Self-made men didn't have to put up with incompetence, and I was no longer competent—at anything. I couldn't even talk right. Most people spoke in phrases or sentences. The words came out of my mouth one at a time at a low pitch, as if I were inebriated or a stroke victim three times my age.

If I stayed in the hospital, I could continue my craft projects, which I didn't admit were really Peggy's projects. Continually telling me I was doing it all by myself, she steadied my hand while we painted the paint-by-number prints of Blue Boy and Pinkie that now hang in my bedroom.

Peggy's Irish smile made life worth living. When I was almost ready to go home, she planned an experimental trip off the hospital grounds.

"Let's go shopping," she urged. "We'll spend a few hours in the city—with *no* wheelchair. You can lean on my shoulder. I'll hold your waist, and we'll just look like two pals walking down the street."

I laughed at the absurdity of the scene. One look in the mirror told me that no one would think I was normal.

"Oh, I don't think so," I protested. "I can't be seen like this. My bones stick out. My eye sockets look like watering holes. I don't move—I jerk and shake." I pictured myself trying to sign a check in this condition. The scrawl would have looked like a preschooler's.

"But you *love* to shop. You haven't been in a store for one and a half years. You have to see the new styles. Max Factor and I will fix up your face."

For a day, Peggy's confidence was almost contagious. She held my fingers still and filed and painted my nails. She washed and put my long hair in a twist. She ran her fingertips, covered with make-up, across my face and highlighted my sunken eyes with color. I felt *almost* normal.

I walked out of the hospital doors to the car and listened to her chatter.

"Isn't this wonderful?"

Yes, but it used to be so much better.

"You can do it."

Yes, but—it takes so much effort.

"I can't wait until I get you downtown."

But—nothing is going to look good on me.

"Come *on*," she would laugh in protest as she tenderly dragged me down the city streets, giving me a day I then viewed as a whiff of a life I didn't want any part of; yet I remember it as if it were sunshine in the midst of a forty-day rain.

Peggy talked me into buying some perfume and a compact, but the bittersweet bottled fragrance hurled me back to the carefree days when I laughed and talked with friends. The memories of men pursuing me had turned on me. Now every man I saw seemed to be laughing at me. I held onto Peggy's waist and inwardly told an unknown God that I could *not* take life if this is what it meant.

Too soon, the doctor said I was ready to go home. I watched Peggy pack my few clothes and toiletries. "I just don't want to go," I stated flatly. "I'm afraid. I failed them. They sent me here to get better. I'm going home worse off."

I looked down into my lap and started to cry.

What *would* Dad say to his Linda, no longer "light"?

Alone, he came to pick me up.

"Hi, Dad," I flashed a beauty-queen smile I hoped would cover a multitude of sins.

"Hello." Nervously his eyes glanced toward but not into mine. He asked a few businesslike questions, said Mom and the girls were fine, then got on to the details of my discharge. Papers had to be signed. Files had to be closed—and all efficiently and quickly, as if he were washing his hands of some unpleasantness.

Peggy cried, and I sniffled as we said our goodbys and waited for Dad to bring the car to the front door of the hospital.

He seemed as awkward with my wheelchair as I would be under the hood of a Camaro. He opened the car door for me, wheeled me to the edge of the seat, then stood back, not knowing what to do next. As always when I did not want the chair to take off on its own, I pushed the handbrake tight against the rubber tire, then I pulled myself up by grabbing onto the frame of the car and plopped myself onto the passenger's front seat. Dad stayed on the sidewalk, not knowing what to do next. "Dad, take off those brakes," I instructed.

He managed that.

"Now lift the chair slightly and push the armrests toward each other."

Awkwardly he followed my instructions and placed the chair upright on the floor of the back seat. He closed my door, climbed in next to me, and turned on the ignition—and the radio.

The ten-minute ride to our house was occupied with listening to music, advertisements, and weather reports, not with the conversation I had both dreaded and longed for but not allowed myself to expect.

I wanted to shout *Do you love me?* over and over until he had no choice but to notice me and give me an answer. But the strength wasn't in me, and besides, I was afraid to know the truth.

Linda, I love you anyway might just as well have been a concept expressible only in Greek, a language foreign to my father's understanding.

We pulled into the driveway to the welcome sight of bouncy Mom, followed by Janet and Billie—all as enthusiastic as baseball fans at a World Series. Mother hugged and kissed me. Janet beamed and hovered. Five-year-old Billie jumped up and down like a yo-yo and ushered me across the patio through the doorway at the back of the house.

The instant I rolled across the threshold, I breathed in the foretaste of Mom's homecoming present: a roast-beef dinner nearly ready to serve. "You sure know how to do things right, Mom," I said, relieved that I could count on her to reduce this day's pain as much as she knew how. But the effect of her mothering softened the next blow about as much as two aspirin could kill the pain of a leg being cut off with a dull saw.

Dad followed us into the living room, but didn't

participate in the celebration. Out of the corner of my eye, I saw him walk to the far end of the hallway flanked by bedrooms. Once inside the den, he closed the door on the sight he couldn't face.

Something in my mind flicked off. That minute I started closing my mind to the world I could only be half part of. If I couldn't have everything, I would have nothing.

4 Escape

"Mom, where's Dad?" I asked after not seeing him for three days. Was he coming home at night after I went to bed and leaving before I got up? Was he not coming home at all? Was I repulsive enough to force him out of the house? After all, I *had* kicked him out of his bedroom. Because it and its adjoining bathroom were more accessible to my wheelchair, Mom had given me the master bedroom. Maybe he thought I was imposing on his territory.

I asked Mom a second time. *"Where is he?"*

"I don't know," she answered, and for a moment she stopped her vegetable chopping and stared off into space. I could see she was telling the truth, and I wished I hadn't asked the question.

If I had known then that she and Dad had been having marital difficulties for some time, I would have been better able to cope with Dad's disappearance. But we were a family of secret-keepers; no one wanted to share his or her private hell with the others. Like C.S. Lewis's queen Orual, we lived behind veils we hoped would hide our blemishes—even from ourselves.

As Mom kept her pain from me, I kept mine from her. I did not openly accuse Dad of leaving because I had come home. I just secretly started making plans to exit from the scene. If I were dead, I wouldn't have to face a worthless life. If I were dead, everyone else's existence would return to normal.

As well as Dad's absence (for which I believed myself responsible) filling Mom's heart with pain, my presence filled her hours with mothering as intense as taking care of a young child.

By day she fattened me up with eggnog and watched television with me—the daily soap operas and sit-coms, "Gomer Pyle" and "Green Acres"—played cards with me, and helped me with my exercises. With the help of Billie and Janet, she was my emotional support. My old friends? I didn't want to see them. I didn't want them to see me. If the door bell rang, I rolled as fast as I could to my room and shut the door behind me. If someone came I had to see, I situated myself on the couch and closeted the wheelchair. I was not about to inflict the sight of myself on anyone (or was it that I didn't want to risk anyone's rejection?). If I said I didn't want to see anyone, I simply didn't have to face any awkward questions . . . or stares . . . or backs turned toward me.

At night Mom rescued me from the larger-than-life horrors that haunted my sleep. "Linda, wake up," she would say as she tried to shake the nightmare from my head and bring me back to reality.

Time after time I woke up crying. The dreams were always similar. Like a child whose parents had sold her into slavery, I was abandoned. Cast off. As good as dead to anyone who loved me.

Dad was gone. Although Mom was with me now, I nightly relived her and Ben's "abandonment" of me in the lobby of the state hospital. No one had seen me through the long bedridden days. No one had held me as the reality of MS had sunk into my consciousness.

I was thoroughly convinced that no one understood my helplessness. Mom frequently said she did, and with increasingly great fervor, I insisted she didn't. "You can't have any idea what I'm going through. You can walk. You can drive a car. You don't have to fear some old friend might see you and gasp. You can do anything you please. I can only sit here." I pounded the palms of my hands against the armrests of my chair, wishing my hands were sledge hammers that would smash my cage to bits.

Being unable to drive and unable to manage stairs were the two curses I found most intolerable. The physical freedom that every walking person takes for granted was stripped from me.

The first time I sat at the bottom of a full flight of stairs and looked up to where I wanted to be, I felt as if I were a lone pioneer facing the wide Missouri River. No ferry in sight. No help within shouting distance. I was more fortunate than many handicapped people: I could crawl up stairs if necessary. But that was no consolation. I had known freedom, and the memory of it made me chafe at my immobility. Inwardly, if not outwardly, I raged.

In an attempt to distract me from my brooding, Mom would ask me to ride across town with her. At the store, she would say, "I'll just be one second." She and Billie would disappear into a building flooded with Muzak while I would turn the car radio on at full volume. The Beatles and the Beach Boys would turn the parking lot into a dance floor where I was the person everyone had stopped to watch. When one song was over, applause thundered across the parking lot until another song started, to which I slowly made love to my imagination's lover.

Then Mom would appear, apologetic, her arms filled with purchases. When she arrived I turned down the radio, allowing myself the luxury of defiance only in her absence. *How can she know the loss I feel?* I had not only felt rejected; I had lost my independence and freedom. I had even been neutered. A man would look at me again only in my daydreams.

Everything . . . everything was gone.

Dead—exactly where I wanted to be. But how? I couldn't aim well enough to slash my wrists. Pills were too risky; I didn't know how many would do the trick, and my cache was limited. I carefully devised a plan to drown myself in the bathtub. I could manage bathing alone. I sat on a low stool next to the tub and swung my legs over the side. Then, by steadying myself on the side of the tub and pulling on the soap dish, I shifted my weight into the water and proceeded to wash. If all went well, my drowning might even look like an accident. They would say I had slipped and then wouldn't be burdened with the stigma of suicide.

Today I'll do it, I told myself for weeks on end. *Today I'll rid the family of their one liability and rid myself of this hell on earth. Today it will work.*

But every day the same scenario was repeated: Just as I had built up enough will power to plunge my head under the layer of bubbles, one of the family walked in to keep me company. Billie popped in to play dolls on the bathroom floor. Or Janet thought of something she had to tell me. Or Mom plunked down on the three-legged stool for a coffee break.

"Why don't you guys just leave me alone?" I growled.

Once interrupted, I could not muster the courage to go through with it until the next day. And then one of the three females lapsed back into her habit of wandering in; it was almost as if their checkups were orchestrated by a Master Conductor.

Who knows the ways God has prepared for us, the people He sets in our paths when we need them most?

As well as staying my self-destructive hand, He sent me a neighbor bearing a gift more precious than any wrapped parcel.

Ruth, a neighbor my mother's age, knew something of suffering. Because she cared for her sick mother, she was more sensitive than most people to the burden I carried and the extra load I put on my mother. Ruth was a Christian, and, although her witness was low-key, her light shone steadily. One day she gave Mom a copy of *The Living New Testament,* with the suggestion that I might find it helpful. The pages of the book were divided with a bookmark, which "just happened" to be placed at the beginning of the Gospel of John.

Mother told me about Ruth's thoughtfulness and laid the book on my dresser. It stayed there until one afternoon when boredom drove me to pick it up. I began reading at the marker to the accompaniment of Top-Forty radio:

Before anything else existed, there was Christ, with God. He has always been alive and is himself God. He created everything there is—nothing exists that he didn't make. Eternal life is in him, and this life gives light to all mankind. His life is the light that shines through the darkness—and the darkness can never extinguish it. God sent John the Baptist as a witness to the fact that Jesus Christ is the true Light. (John 1:1–7 LB)

After reading a few pages I thought, *This is pretty good but not for me,* and I put the paperback aside. Yet within a few weeks I was playing games with myself, trying to find comforting passages that would momentarily give me hope, a reason to keep on going.

Although I had no understanding that the Gospels might be telling a true story, I knew they were describing someone I would like to meet, someone I wished existed. The Jesus described by Matthew, Mark, Luke, and John would not turn His back on someone who couldn't walk. He had touched unclean people, healed every hurt He saw (and some He didn't see), and loved with a supernatural constancy. This character's love was blind, like a perfect father's, something I could appreciate only since the onset of my illness.

If this guy were alive, He would understand me, I thought, and suddenly I had a new, imaginary friend who knew where I was coming from. If only He were real. . . .

"Mom," I said one morning, "you should try this book; you might like it." Her eyes were growing more hollow every day. Although she was only forty-seven, she walked as if her shoulders carried all ninety-five pounds of me.

"Oh, it's for you, honey. I don't think I'd be much interested. But I'll read it to you, if you like."

She didn't read me the Bible. But somewhere she picked up a thick devotional book on prayer and read me a selection each morning. The long-forgotten author of the devotional obviously believed that God and Jesus were alive. But that thought was beyond my spiritual understanding. The seeds that were being sown needed time to germinate and grow. One thing I knew: If He *were* alive, I was mad at Him for getting me into this mess.

The weeks that followed were a roller-coaster ride of emotions—despair that sent me bathing until I looked like a prune; anger that, in consideration of Mom, I tried to keep bottled; and denial of reality that sent me into near nymphomaniacal trances. And also it propelled me to try to walk the hallway from den to living room. With enough practice, I *would* prove the pamphlets wrong. *I am in control,* I would convince myself. Physical degeneration and I were not going to be bedfellows, not even acquaintances.

But then the hopelessness of it all would crash down on me, and I would know there was no where to run—or walk—or even roll.

At precisely 4:30 each morning I woke. The woodpecker that banged his beak against the downspout outside my window didn't know the hour was a sacred one among human sleepers. Those who call themselves night owls are surely tucked away by 4:00 A.M., while early risers rarely venture out before 5:00. Nor did the woodpecker know the futility of his labors. As the weeks came and went, he never bored a hole through the metal tubing.

It seemed he pecked just for my benefit, to remind me there was life outside the four walls of home.

One morning his rhythmic alarm awoke me right on schedule. *Another day,* I groggily thought. *Another day of the same intolerable routine. I can't even manage to drown myself. What can I do for myself?*

I couldn't think of anything.

Then what can I do for Mom?

You can make Dad come home.

Yes, but how? I had tried everything I knew. *Maybe praying would work.*

But I don't know how to pray.

I thought of what Mom and I had read in the devotional and took a big leap. If God had got me into this and if God were love, He could get me out of it. "Lord, You know how rotten this situation is and how badly I need to get out of here. Please, *do* something—if not for me, for Mom. Do something that will make Dad come home."

Eventually the woodpecker gave up and went to find more satisfying food. I waited for the rest of the family to stir, wondering if anyone had heard my request.

The day progressed like any other. I went to bed that night, still doubting the existence of life above the clouds. I hadn't seen any miracles; no one must have heard. With a sigh of resignation I reminded myself that only children believe in fairy tales.

But bigger surprises than I had imagined came at the end of the week, though I didn't initially perceive them as such.

Mom's sister, Bonnie, came from California to visit. She, Mom, and Dad cooked up a proposal they did not want me to refuse. One afternoon Mom knocked on the door of my room where I was holed-up with a book and a radio, escaping their tedious older-generation conversation.

"Come out to the den, honey. We want to ask you something." She wheeled me out, and I was greeted by Aunt Bonnie who was glowing and Dad who was glowering.

Mom did the talking: "We have the best news, Linda. Bonnie wants you to go out and live with her and Ernie for a while. It will give you a change, new scenery."

Oh, where, oh, where had "Light" Linda gone? The idea of travel, of new places, and new faces set about as well with me as roast pork on a queasy stomach. "Really?" I coolly responded as Mom sat on the edge of her chair and enthusiastically filled me in on the details.

"I'll think about it," I mumbled before rolling myself back to my solitude.

Once alone, I saw things more clearly. I had been looking at the scheme as a child, too young to understand the intricacies of chess, looks at a board holding a half-finished game. There seemed no purpose to the pattern and no reason for any next move. But I began to realize which piece should take the next leap and in which direction.

Here's the chance I've been waiting for, I thought, suddenly excited about the prospect before me. *If I move out, maybe Dad will move back in.* He had begun coming to the house in the daytime. Surely all that was keeping him away at night was my presence. I would go to California. He would have his bedroom, and life for Mom would return to normal.

With my sights set on a new life, I headed west.

I didn't even pause for a second to thank God for leading me out of the dry pasture; having forgotten I had requested this escape route, I just packed my bags and left.

I was the first to board the Boeing 727 that would deliver me, ready for life, to Los Angeles.

Almost overnight I had turned a page scribbled with ugly, destructive graffiti to write symbols of hope on a clean white page. I convinced myself I was again beautiful and—although slightly under-weight—still a sight to behold.

Janet had done my nails and, with a little help from a cluster-of-curls hair piece, had almost returned my locks to their former glory. Once I was settled in my window seat and the wheelchair out of sight, I would look like—no, better than—any other passenger.

Who will sit next to me? I wondered.

I had chosen a rear seat as close as possible to the plane's engines, carefully calculating that their noise would drown out the imperfections of my voice.

The seat was filled with one hunk of a soldier. His crew cut did his looks little disservice. I could just picture him with a full head of hair—something worth writing home about.

Just as I used to, I would turn it all on and knock him off his chair.

I waited until we were off the ground and firmly on our way.

"Where are you from?" I inquired in my most provocative voice, not turning my head so as to avoid appearing overeager.

He didn't answer. I repeated the question, this time a little louder.

Silence.

He can't do this, I thought. *He can't just pretend I'm not here. I'll try again,* and with all the charm I could muster, I repeated the question.

He didn't move a muscle.

I could hardly contain myself. I wanted to wring my hands around his neck. *He has no right—no right to treat me like a nobody. Doesn't he know I was one of the most beautiful women in the country? Doesn't he know . . . ?*

Above the purr of the engines, I heard the unmistakable grunt of a snore, and relief, like the sudden cold-water gush from a shower nozzle, washed away the heat of my anger.

His sleep immediately redefined, even absolved, his rudeness; his sleep gave me a second chance to prove my prowess. I would regroup and try again after lunch.

We ate in silence. Only after I had checked the state of my make-up in my compact mirror did I ask my cocktail-party question: "Where are you from?"

As kind as a mother to a sick child he answered, "Atlanta." Then, in a drawl that proved his truth-telling, he returned the question, "And you?"

I half covered my mouth with my hand and said, "Topeka. Have you been in the service long?"

"No, ma'am. They just nabbed me."

After a conversation that lasted less than a full minute, the private closed his eyes and returned to his world of dreams, where he stayed until we descended into Los Angeles.

For the remaining hour of the trip I gloated in my victory; I had fooled him. *I haven't lost it,* I told myself. *It's obvious that he's interested. He's even comfortable with me—comfortable enough to know that he doesn't have to talk all the time.* (Sometimes it's good just to fall asleep next to someone. It's kind of like a vote of confidence; letting someone see you in your most vulnerable state.)

When the doors finally opened and let in the warm Los Angeles air, he jumped up. With a quick "Nice talking with you, ma'am," he was gone.

But his nonexistent attention bolstered me for days. A stranger had met me apart from my tyrannical keeper, my wheelchair, and had treated me as I had been treated in old times. Things were looking up. I was ready for California. Was California ready for me?

Only years later did I view that flight in realistic terms: a polite young soldier had tried to spare me—or himself—embarrassment. He may have been tired, but what would have better prevented him from saying the wrong thing (how frequently people squirm when faced with someone physically less fortunate than themselves) to me, so obviously handicapped (no wheelchair clue was needed to guess that secret), than feigning sleep? Not wanting to draw attention to my less-than-graceful table manners, he had not talked during lunch. Not wanting to witness my wheelchair enslavement, he had quickly left the plane. Desperation had transformed what once would have been a slap in my face—someone preferring sleep to my company—into an ego boost. He *had* spoken to me. He had shown no sign of revulsion.

Not then, nor ever after, did I fool anyone but myself into thinking I was physically what I once had been. But for a moment, when I faced the challenge of California with no inner strength except what I could pull up from within myself, I had to preserve my ego—at any cost.

The new life called for a new outlook. Whether it was true or not, I, like the little-engine-that-could, believed. Nothing else mattered.

5 My Hope for Years to Come

When I looked from the window of the bedroom I shared with my twelve-year-old cousin, Jena, I drank in the excitement of Hollywood. The studios' hubbub was under cover, but the famous sign that covers the hillside never let me forget where I was.

Day after perfect day I soaked in the sun that hit Aunt Bonnie's back yard, browning my face and legs copper while I read a breed of book I had newly discovered: self-improvement.

I'm O.K., You're O.K. was followed by *Psycho-Cybernetics, The Magic Power of Self-Image Psychology,* and then the one I nearly memorized, Norman Vincent Peale's *Tough-Minded Optimist.*

To reenergize my body, I ate local oranges nearly the size of softballs. To enhance my social life, I started going to meetings of the Multiple Sclerosis Society. To enlarge my mind, I enrolled in a journalism course at Cypress Junior College. I read the self-help books as religiously as I now read the Bible, and they nearly convinced me that the world was at my fingertips. *I just had to reach out and grasp it.*

The monthly MS meetings were interesting—entertainment, refreshments, news of the latest research, and conversation with fellow patients—but I quickly decided to view my junior-college classmates as potential friends. Many of the MS patients were older and more debilitated than I, married, and prone to complain—not the kind of friends I would need if I were to concentrate on the positive. I wanted to be supportive of the group but, in short, did not want to spend evenings in depressing talk. Life was too short for that.

School was my answer. It was not within rolling distance, nor could I depend on Aunt Bonnie for transportation. So I placed an ad in the school paper. It worked. A ride was always available for hire. Getting around campus without a battery-powered chair was difficult but manageable. I paddled my feet along, like a duck swimming through water.

As the semester progressed, I gathered friends around me who were surprisingly blind to my handicap. I met many at my hangout, the student-affairs office.

One morning the secretary-receptionist went out of her way to catch my attention. "Hi." She buoyantly interrupted my diligent search through a stack of papers. The one I was looking for was, of course, near the bottom of the pile.

"Hi," I mumbled, not even bothering to look up.

"Beautiful day," she persisted.

"Uh huh," I agreed.

"My name is Launa Nygren."

Some quality in her voice was irresistible. I stopped my shuffling and turned toward her.

"You're Linda, aren't you?" Her smile matched her pleasant voice.

"Yes, but I don't think we've met. How do you know me?"

"I've heard there was a new MS student, and I've been eager to meet you. My mother-in-law has MS, so I have some interest in how you're progressing. I know what a struggle it can be."

After several conversations, Launa invited me to her home for dinner. At her apartment I was greeted by a handsome man with a radiant countenance akin to Launa's. It was her husband, Ron. He escorted me into the comfortable but not luxurious living room. The first thing I saw was a portrait of Jesus above the mantel; the second thing, a plaque on the far wall reading: "Love is patient. Love is kind."

With a glint of pride in his voice, Ron introduced me to a stranger in the room, "Linda, this is my sister Patti." Patti rose from her fireside seat and extended her hand to me. Her face radiated that same undefinable something.

Launa appeared from the kitchen and led us to the dining room, where we settled around the table, eager to devour the feast she had prepared.

I picked up my napkin, spread it in my lap, and sipped the water from my glass, patiently waiting for Launa to pass me the food, but Ron softly announced that he would say a blessing. I didn't remember ever sitting through grace before, but it was obviously a treasured ritual at this table.

Ron addressed God as if He were sitting among us. "Father, bless this food. And a special thanks for our dinner guest. Cover her with Your love and comfort and use us as instruments of Your grace. In Jesus' name. Amen."

Immediately Launa handed me the dish of potatoes. I simply filed the pause for prayer in the back of my mind until after dinner when Ron openly confronted me with the faith that had prompted it. "Linda, we want to share our faith in Christ with you," he stated matter-of-factly.

I wasn't put off by his boldness but rather perked up like a wilted flower after a rain.

"All three of us have suffered hardship, and through our suffering, God has drawn us to Himself. Knowing God and His Son, Jesus, has made all the difference in our lives. The knowledge that Jesus died for our sins gave us new life. Our faith in His dying for us and giving us eternal life gives us daily strength. That same eternal life is offered to you, Linda. All you have to do is believe in Jesus' taking the penalty for your sin— He died in your place—and the gift of eternal life is yours."

I swallowed hard. Did this have something to do with these people's happiness, their gentleness, their low-key acceptance of me?

I listened but didn't answer the indirect question. Later, however, I accepted Patti's invitation to accompany her to the beach to soak up more of California's best commodity: sunshine.

Patti took me to the shore several times, and after we had become good friends, she informed me that she wanted me to meet her mother, Jerri, whose MS, she warned, was severely advanced.

"Sure," I agreed, even though I didn't feel up to spending time with someone who was worse off than myself.

Patti's mother, Jerri, was virtually motionless, unable to move from her green leather chair, but her face seemed to glow. Like Ron, she came directly to the point of her spiritual concern for me. "Patti tells me you have a lot of spiritual questions. Is there anything I can help you with?"

How can this woman, truly a prisoner in her own body, offer me help? The prospect of it sent me into a tailspin. I couldn't think of a thing to say. "Uh," I stammered like a kindergartner on the first day of school. "Who does your hair?"

The question I really wanted to ask, "How can you have such peace when you can't even move?" had been lost in the confusion of my mind.

"I have a beautician come in once a week," she answered graciously.

A short silence followed. I could tell Jerri was listening to the lyrics of the music playing on the radio near her chair:

Something beautiful, something good—
All my confusion He understood;
All I had to offer Him was brokenness and strife,
But He made something beautiful of my life.

I listened also until Jerri continued her conversation with me: "Do you know Jesus as your Lord and Savior? He *has* made something beautiful of my life."

And I could see that He had. Jerri—and Launa, Ron, and Patti—had something I needed, but I still was not able to ask the right questions or to fully accept what they were claiming as the source of their peace and joy.

Little did I know He was at my door, waiting for me to open it and let Him in.

> "Here I am! I stand at the door and knock. If anyone hears my voice and opens the door, I will come in and eat with him, and he with me." (Revelation 3:20)

Launa was not the only Christian I met at the student union. I frequently ate lunch with Laurie, and she introduced me to her friends Jennifer and Beth. Their faith was not often mentioned, but the same joy permeated the atmosphere when I was with them. They, too, had something I didn't. Something beautiful inside of them.

One midweek afternoon Laurie called me at home.

"Tonight we're going to a Billy Graham Crusade at Anaheim Stadium. Wanna come with us?"

I *wanted* to stay home. The Beach Boys were giving a TV concert, which I had been looking forward to for weeks. Billy Graham in person didn't seem like any competition for the Beach Boys on screen, but then, it wasn't every night that friends asked me out. Turning down an invitation from friends I really liked was a gamble, I calculated, and that, alone, was the determining factor. I went.

The baseball park was crawling with spectators—some looking as if heaven could be no better than this. Some, like me, looked as if they had just come along for the ride. Laurie, Jennifer, and Beth sat with me, in a special wheelchair section, right on the playing field. Immediately, I started kidding them: "So this is why you brought me along. Just so you could get good seats. You could have just borrowed my wheelchair, you know, and one of you could have sat in it."

"You can't get away with that, Linda," they teased in return until the choir and the fans started belting out "Blessed Assurance," a song I had never heard.

When the sun had finished its long day's work, the stars took their shift, sprinkling the sky with specks of light. When the singing died down, Dr. Graham opened his oversized Bible and read a passage I now know to be from Romans 8, including the verse he used as his sermon text: "And we know that in all things God works for the good of those who love him, who have been called according to his purpose" (v. 28).

Throughout most of the sermon, my skeptical nature firmly held its ground. This stuff may have worked for Jerri, but she was different. The little spiritual headway I had gained in the last few weeks was suddenly gone. This just couldn't be true. If Laurie had leaned over and asked, "What do you think?" and if I had had the courage to be completely honest with her, I would have answered, "This is a bunch of baloney. God may be up there, but what does Billy Graham know about life this side of that podium? Life down here on the playing field is worlds away from the God he's talking about who lives among those twinkling stars. By pulling at my bootstraps, things have become better than disastrous, but with no thanks to God."

Life for me was a three on a scale of one to ten. I was beginning to think I had been a little too ambitious in taking on the journalism course; my energy level, despite those colossal oranges, frequently dragged me to a halt. Life was okay but a long way from good, and if God had good in mind for me, where was it?

But somewhere during point three of the presentation, the Word of God, like a sword, penetrated my thoughts. What Ron and Patti had been telling me seemed to fit in with what Dr. Graham was saying.

Maybe He is real and concerned about me; maybe He's waiting for me to give Him a chance; maybe He has something He wants me to see.

When the choir started singing "Just As I Am," Laurie leaned over and asked if I wanted to go forward and pray.

I did, but the matter was a private one, something I had to do for myself. I wanted to go to God alone, under my own power. As I paddled across the grass, I listened to the words of the song. They were words written for a beauty queen fallen from her pedestal, for a handicapped woman growing weary of proving herself, for a little girl still hoping that a father loved her no matter what.

They were also words for the hundreds of other people who joined me in a prayer acknowledging our helplessness and acceptance of God's grace of forgiving love. With open arms, Jesus was calling us children to Himself:

> *Just as I am, without one plea*
> *But that Thy blood was shed for me,*
> *And that Thou bid'st me come to Thee,*
> *O Lamb of God, I come! I come!*

> *Just as I am, and waiting not*
> *To rid my soul of one dark blot,*
> *To thee whose blood can cleanse each spot,*
> *O Lamb of God, I come! I come!*

> *Just as I am, tho tossed about*
> *With many a conflict, many a doubt,*
> *Fightings and fears within, without,*
> *O Lamb of God, I come! I come!*

> *Just as I am, poor, wretched, blind—*
> *Sight, riches, healing of the mind,*
> *Yea, all I need in Thee to find—*
> *O Lamb of God, I come! I come!*

> *Just as I am, Thou wilt receive,*
> *Wilt welcome, pardon, cleanse, relieve;*
> *Because Thy promise I believe,*
> *O Lamb of God, I come! I come!*

That night the sprouts of the seeds God had planted and carefully preserved broke through the ground. A seedling Christian was growing in the light of the Son. But as a baby understands little of life, I had an infant's understanding of what I had done. All the way home in the car, Laurie, Jennifer, and Beth answered questions as basic as a pagan's. Exactly what did it mean? How would life as a Christian be different?

"Jesus lives inside you, now," said Laurie. "You

belong to Him; He belongs to you. He has made you a new person."

I looked from one face to the other. They all nodded in unison.

I felt somewhat bewildered, like a child who had arrived at the right answer to a difficult math problem, but didn't really know how.

"The Lord will mold your attitudes and reactions to align with His perspective. The change will be an inner one." Laurie continued her explanations in a low, reassuring voice.

I nodded my head in dubious agreement.

They were careful not to make sweeping statements of how rosy life was going to be, yet I went to bed hoping that I would wake up and be able to hop out of it as I once had. God was going to work everything for the good, wasn't He? I had been called to be one of His, and what, short of walking, could be defined in such encouraging terms?

But when the next morning dawned, I was physically no better off than I had been the night before. From the edge of my bed, I pulled myself to a standing position. Then, to see what good God had made of me, I let go of the headboard.

The mattress cushioned what would have been a solid "kerplunk" onto the floor, and my twelve-hour-old understanding of the good life lost its shape, like a balloon out of air.

I loaded all my disappointments onto a cart and dumped them at the feet of my local expert on matters of faith, Laurie. "It didn't work for me," I said. "Things aren't any better for me today than they were yesterday."

With great patience, over a period of weeks, Laurie and Jennifer unfolded secrets of the faith: "We're in progress, like children becoming adults, like bolts of fabric being cut and sewn into garments, like iron ore being refined and melted into steel girders. Who are we, the creation, to tell the Designer, the Architect what would be the most beautiful or most useful place for us? The end result of God's good design for each of us is being made Christlike, and because each of us is a unique person, the process to His perfection is different for each one. Only God knows what 'good' means for Linda."

Christlike. From Ruth's New Testament I remembered images of Jesus' life. I liked Him. Although I thought of it rarely, and only vaguely, I knew "I really like who I am" was not something I had ever been able to say—despite my pride, even bravado. As a teenager I had occasionally sat at my vanity, looked into the mirror, and wished . . . wished I had been more likable.

Christlike. That's what I wanted to be—at least in my head. It would be years before the reality of what that meant traveled throughout my whole system.

The rigors of school proved more than I could handle. Before the end of the semester I dropped the course, but not my friends, who accompanied me to their Bible studies and encouraged me in my new interest—fund raising for the MS Society.

Casey Howell, the director of the Southern California Chapter, phoned me frequently. His request was always the same: "Linda, we really could use someone with your experience, your background, and your smile to make the public more aware of what we're fighting."

"But—my voice—"

"We'll give you a mike. They'll understand you perfectly. The few who don't won't miss what that smile of yours says."

Casey was right about the smile. I had too often misplaced it, but it was the one thing I hadn't lost, and it did help his cause—raising money for research.

A thousand soldiers at the El Toro Naval Air Base didn't know they were guinea pigs. They were the first to sit through my post-MS attempts at public speaking. I thanked God that a bank of potted plants separated me from the audience and that the auditorium's lights were so dim I couldn't see the onlookers.

Casey, a jovial Santa-sort, accompanied me, playing the role Mom always had. "You're going to do just fine," he assured me, as if he had some secret knowledge of the future. Despite my apprehension, his words of encouragement and my friends' prayers for strength and composure paid off—that night's MS rally raised more dollars per person than any to date in that region.

Since the day of my conversion, Romans 8:28— all things working for the good—had roamed around inside my head, looking for a place to be comfortable. God must have had a hand in guiding Ruth to give me that New Testament. And He must have wanted me in California. Did this and my efforts for the MS Society have something to do with God's good?

It seemed so. It provided me with work and with personal and practical goals—both important to life. My existence mattered, not only to a God whom I couldn't see, not only to a small circle of friends whom I needed more than they needed me, but to thousands of sick people, many of whom were more handicapped—physically and emotionally—than I.

Someone, at least Casey Howell, still thought I was beautiful, talented, and useful as a representative of those who suffered the effects of MS.

One of Casey's phone calls in the spring of 1970 took me off guard. I was expecting the usual request: Would I tell my story to a local group.

But Casey had grander designs. "I've mentioned you to the national organization, and they feel you are the perfect person to appoint the honorary chairwoman of this year's fund-raising campaign. How would you feel about going to Washington, D.C., and making a presentation to Mrs. Nixon at a tea in the library of the White House? We've discussed it at length and feel you're exactly the right person."

The embarrassment that had sent me to my room a few years earlier when the doorbell rang had slowly washed away. The old saying "success breeds success" had proven true. I had made other public appearances; I would make this one. I would meet the wife of the president with my head high. The room would be small (no faceless audience here), and the setting intimate. (Something seemed absurd about trying to arrange my seating in front of an air conditioner to muffle my voice.) Although the ceremony would honor Mrs. Nixon, I chose to view my having been selected to go to the White House as an honor of its own.

Besides saying a few magic words—"I hereby appoint you to be the honorary chairperson of our campaign"—I presented Mrs. Nixon, younger, lovelier, and more gracious than I had ever imagined, with a copy of the National Multiple Sclerosis Society's annual report. The cover had a composite photo of me—before and after MS. Along with the job came the publicity of being the MS poster girl—and that idea didn't thrill me.

Pity was something I could live without. I was well-enough aware of what I had lost without having the country stare at me and shake their heads and say, "Isn't it pathetic." The public, I thought, would put me in the same corner of their minds as they put Jerry Lewis's yearly handicapped child—doomed to a hard-times life, in need of sympathy.

Attention I had lived with, even craved. Understanding friends—who could have too many? And an occasional tablespoon (or even cupful) of pity from a relative (especially Mom), I delighted in. But pity and patronizing, which set me up as the victim and every Tom, Dick, and Mary as my savior, seemed a destructive force.

As an older person, who had worked all her life and always paid her own way, doesn't like to take charity from anyone, I struggled with allowing my then-and-now pictures to be plastered, like pictures of carnival freaks, in grocery stores and libraries from Maine to Oregon.

I discussed my feelings with Casey. What did he think I should do? Was I being oversensitive?

Casey's reasoning was clear and simple: "Look at the good you'll do. You're not asking for money for yourself but for the thousands of people who can't do it for themselves. And you're not only fund raising; you're helping us publicize the early symptoms that will warn people they should see a doctor. Think of yourself—if you'd been better informed and had known what questions to ask a doctor, you might have been spared . . . considerable heartache."

There was no sense in dwelling on "if onlys," especially when the passing of time had brought so many changes. MS had always been difficult to diagnose, but in the seven years since 1963 when my symptoms had become evident, and even since 1966 when my MS had been diagnosed, researchers had unearthed a mine of information. More people had MS than was previously thought. Many early cases were self-diagnosed, like my own, and credited to having gotten up on the wrong side of the bed. Many mild cases remained inactive for years before causing any debilitating flare-ups. Because of the here-today, gone-tomorrow nature of the symptoms, a lot of people chose to ignore early warnings such as fatigue, clumsiness, and numb, tingling, or shaky hands. MS is still difficult to pinpoint and is shrouded in mystery. Its cause is unknown. It may be a virus (though surely not contagious), but the evidence is not conclusive. Why is it most prevalent in temperate, not tropical, zones? Why is it so fickle in its effects? Many combinations of its symptoms can also be symptoms of other illnesses, so all must be documented before a doctor is sure what he or she is dealing with. Now MS is not considered an automatic ticket to a wheelchair, but that feeling was not as widely held ten years ago.

In theory, Casey convinced me that I should do whatever I could to further the research (questions need answers), help support fellow patients, and increase public awareness. But my gut reaction remained unchanged. I would participate by choice, deciding to look at my part in the poster-girl campaign as a responsibility God had placed in my path, and I posed for those pictures exuding just as much healthy pride as I had once posed with unhealthy pride. Just as I was—I would do my part.

The poster-girl campaign and the publicized trip to the White House prompted the editors of *Parade* magazine to take note. They featured me in a story on what had become of various ex-beauty queens. Across the country men and women glanced at my before-and-after pictures and then threw away the magazine supplement of a September Sunday paper in 1970. That is, all except one man who found the story that described me as "spunky" particularly fascinating. For no logical reason he folded up the photo and caption and placed it, like a valued keepsake, in his billfold where it lay almost forgotten for three years.

Something
Beautiful

86

On the flight west from Washington, D.C., I collected my thoughts and tried to put my life back into perspective. I had spent an hour at the White House chatting with the first lady. Despite my having been nervous for the twenty-four hours I had been in the capital city (*Would I knock something over or get crumbs on the carpet? Would I slip up on some point of protocol? Would I become tongue-tied and forget my presentation or find conversation with Mrs. Nixon difficult?*), things had gone well. I had shaken Mrs. Nixon's hand in a receiving line, given her the honor, then enjoyed a cup of tea and petits fours and pleasant talk with her. The day had been flawless. I sighed a prayer of thanksgiving for God's steadying hand.

For the last few weeks thoughts of this day had grown bigger and bigger. My flight out of Washington may as well have been Christmas afternoon, and I, a seven-year-old. The thrill was only a memory, and what would replace the anticipation that time had stolen? What work would fill tomorrow?

Surely more speaking for MS, but would that be enough to keep me occupied? I was on my way to a few days off with Carole and Allan, who had moved to Cincinnati, Ohio. In the surroundings of their home they would cheer me up and give me some pointers.

Once I was settled in her home, Carole made the suggestion I half wanted her to: "Why don't you stop in Topeka. Say hello to Mom, and just check things out. When did you go to California—two years ago?"

"Yeah. Billie must be getting so big."

"Dad's back home, and things will be better than they were when you left."

"Oh, I don't know. Those months were so hard. It's masochistic to walk—ha!—back into it again."

"Do you want to see Mom?"

"Sure." Phone conversations with Mom hadn't brought her close enough to me. Only being there—in Topeka—would give me her smile.

Allan put in his two-cents' worth. "I think, for your mom's sake, you should visit for a few days."

And for Mom's sake, I did.

Dad picked me up at the airport and took me home to Mom who again welcomed me with a huge dinner and open arms.

Dad's pain—caused by my condition—was still in his eyes. My pain—caused by what I perceived as his rejection—was still in my veins.

We both tried to hide our wounds and resume our pre-MS dinner talk—who, in Topeka circles of power, was doing what—but not without strain. With suspicion and slight disdain, he watched me out of the corner of his eye. I grew less and less hungry and started to pick at my food, wishing he would hurry and finish eating and go off to his den.

Mom had news of her own. After helping me settle into my old room, she hit me with it: "Bonnie and Ernie are feeling a financial crunch right now and don't feel they can continue to keep up with the expenses of your being there. The Social Security check just isn't enough."

"That means . . ." I hesitated, wanting Mom to answer with some brilliant alternative plan.

"It means we'll have to supplement the check, or you'll have to stay here—and Dad and I've already decided sending them more money is out of the question."

A few weeks of vegetating in Mom's care and staying out of Dad's way was all I could take. A part of me loved Mom's cooing and pampering, but California had opened too many doors for me to stay cooped up for the rest of my life with my mother as my keeper. Other than my problems with Dad, boredom defined one of my frustrations, and dependence, another. My aunt's mention of my upkeep simmered in the back of my mind, like a pot of soup on the back of a stove. If Social Security didn't cover my bills in California, why would it in Kansas? I would have to start thinking about bringing in an income. Being a case for charity was no longer a vague poster-girl issue, but a family one, and my pride was no longer some cosmic self-respect, but a raw, powerfully motivating drive: I had to prove myself.

I was still a young Christian, and most of my praying was of the "God help me" variety. I wanted Him to remove the stones from my path to allow me smooth rolling. My stuck-at-home predicament, therefore, sent me to my bedroom to ask God to turn me toward and give me a push down the least-rocky road.

A few days later, at no one's suggestion, I picked up the phone book. As if directed by the invisible hand of God, my fingers walked straight to the number of the State Vocational Rehabilitation Agency. *That's it,* an inaudible voice whispered. *Call them and tell them you need help.*

For this phone conversation, I knew I needed the extra courage that comes from privacy. The phone in the kitchen was too public. When Dad wasn't home, I made my way into his den. Feeling like an intruding criminal, I turned the door knob and pushed open the door to the room where no one had permission to trespass. I inhaled a stale, musty odor and shivered when hit with the cool of the air-conditioning. There was something evil, almost sinister about this room. I wanted to throw open the windows and allow the fresh air and sunshine to chase away the dingy stifling air.

As I approached my father's desk, I shivered again—but not from the temperature. This place gave me the willies. I dialed the agency number and silently chastised myself for being nervous. *Jesus is at my side—isn't He?*

"Kansas State Vocational Rehabilitation Agency. May I help you?" A cheery voice urged me to make my request.

I haltingly explained my plight and asked if the agency could help.

"I believe so," the woman replied. "Let me refer you to one of our counselors." The line rang into another office.

"Bill Fredrichs. What can I do for you?"

With little hesitation I gave a detailed explanation of my situation; then I asked about the possibility of being trained for a new line of work.

"First, we'd have to administer some aptitude tests to determine your abilities; then we would go from there." I liked this man's easy manner. "I can come out for an interview tomorrow. What would be a convenient time for you?"

He is asking me *about a convenient time?* I had all the time in the world.

We set a time for the next afternoon, and I hung up, thankful that Mr. Fredrichs had made me feel like a worthwhile person. Maybe this *would* work. *Now, let me get out of this room as fast as possible. . . .*

As I pushed myself back from my father's desk, I nearly knocked over an almost empty glass precariously set near the edge. Sure enough, when I reached for it, irritated that he hadn't returned it to the kitchen, it toppled, some of the liquid splashing out. Although diluted with melted ice, the aroma that reached my nostrils was unmistakable: bourbon.

Bourbon! I sat for a moment and stared at the telltale glass. I didn't like what I was thinking. Was this why Dad spent so much time holed-up in his den? Was this an escape from the life he could no longer face? Was this the cause of behavior that seemed so unlike him? The questions were followed by the too familiar guilt feelings I seemed to carry in connection with Dad. Was I to blame for this?

I put my head on the desk and tried to throw off the condemning attack. "Oh, God," I groaned, "please—" My tears defined my plea to my heavenly Father who knows our requests before we even ask. I wanted to be as far from that icy room as I could. I wanted to be rid of the pain it had caused me.

That afternoon's tears may not have washed away my resentments that would flare up for years, but, in that hour, God did reach down and supernaturally erase my irrational guilt. It was as if a highly tensed wire inside me snapped, and I seemed instantly to understand a truth that many people need to be told again and again: *We cannot carry the responsibility for another person's choices.* I was freed from the guilt. When at last the flood of tears had subsided, I picked up the glass, took it to the kitchen, and washed it clean—clean as my conscience and clear as my thoughts.

The next afternoon, Mr. Fredrichs arrived at the front door. Within minutes, the tall, slender career counselor was seated on the couch, asking about my background and interests. My background I could spell out; as to my interests, I tried to throw that ball back to him.

"I don't know what I want to do; that's why I called you. What *can* I do?"

My "I can do anything—I can do nothing" cycles still fluctuated like a sine curve. What people told me about myself I believed. Dad's silent disapproval being my most recent barometer, I thought I might be able to get a job at Goodwill or, if God's idea of good and mine happened to be somewhat aligned, I might be fortunate enough to learn how to weave baskets.

"We'd have to start with some testing to establish your capabilities," Mr. Fredrichs answered. "But, as you thought, we're here to let you know what's available."

After a few minutes he took Mom aside for a private conversation, which she later relayed to me. He asked her if she thought me intellectually quick enough to handle college work.

Mom answered, "She's surely smart enough if she can handle it physically and if she's motivated. She tried in California and getting around campus was too much for her. She tried right out of high school and couldn't see any point to it."

The aptitude test he gave me was not difficult. I wondered what he would have in mind for me when he returned with the results.

"I think we have just the right place for you," he enthusiastically announced a week later. "Emporia State Teachers College."

"Whoa," I said. "I've tried it before and it just doesn't work."

"No. No," he cautioned pleasantly. "Don't discount the idea so quickly. Emporia is different."

"But you forget, I'm twenty-six—too old to fit in with those kids."

"It's an hour's drive away, and later this week my assistant and I are going down to check on my case load. Why don't you come along with us and look the place over? Then you'll have a better idea of what you're dealing with."

I was a pushover for a day out of the house. "Well, it can't hurt," I answered. An out-of-town trip sounded fun, and, besides, I wanted to give God a chance. What if the college at the other end of the road was His answer to my prayer?

At dinner that night the "what can Linda do?" scenario was repeated. But this time it was no stranger who wondered about my capabilities. I was a spectator but not a participant of the conversation that opened with Mom filling Dad in on the day's news. "Bill, the State Rehabilitation Agency thinks Linda should go to college."

Her encouraging words were followed by an uncomfortable and prolonged silence. Finally Dad cleared his throat and looked straight at Mom seated at the far end of the table. The tone of his voice said as much as the words. Incredulity iced over the room as he said, "You really think she can?"

I may as well have been a fly on the wall, not a live member of the family sitting at the table, capable of hearing and feeling. Having been trained well, I didn't say anything. I played with my food, clenched my teeth, and inwardly determined that I would prove him wrong if it killed me. *Just you wait and see,* I thought. *Just—you—wait—and—see.*

At first glance, Emporia looked promising. Ten years ahead of its time, the campus was specially designed for handicapped students—ramps and elevators making every building accessible, and special dorm facilities making personal care manageable, even comfortable. Doorways were wide enough for my chair and many were electronic, like the ones found in grocery stores.

And beautiful? The architect and the landscaper had outdone themselves. The low lines of the stately brick and stone buildings were pleasing even to an untrained eye, and the greenery and lilac bushes that surrounded them were inviting. Many old elm trees had been left in place. A small lake, sporting two fountains and an arched stone pedestrian bridge, graced the center of the campus.

The 1970 version of summer school was in session, and even in late June the self-contained community was bustling. The admissions office filled me in on details: One hundred of their seven thousand students were disabled; some more than I. The dorm we visited, the cafeteria where we ate lunch, the sidewalks I maneuvered all proved these statistics. Accident victims, muscular-dystrophy patients, and other multiple-sclerosis patients were the norm rather than the exception.

This was where I wanted to be.

What would I study? The decision didn't seem terribly important, but I chose what fascinated me: early childhood education.

The only obstacle to my admission popped up at the housing office. There were no rooms suitable for handicapped students available for the fall semester. With little hope of anything opening up, the man behind the executive desk said, "We'll reserve you a place in January and, in case someone backs out, put you on a waiting list for September."

My heart sank. I had quickly established that Emporia was God's answer to my prayer, but He had slipped up on one vital detail. January seemed light-years away. I had wanted to establish my independence now, not next year. I breathed a silent prayer, trying to remove from my mind the dread of six more months of dinners at the same table with Dad. "Lord—you're going to have to get me through those months—"

The expenses? Mr. Fredrichs assured me that the state would pick up my tab. The education, after all, would train me in a new field, my handicap having made modeling and hostessing impossible. The state's support would include their purchase of a battery-powered wheelchair, making daily cross-campus jaunts as easy as flicking a switch. The purchase was no small matter—fifteen hundred dollars—but it was the one piece of equipment that made my Emporia years possible.

Studying seemed infinitely better than working for Goodwill or weaving baskets. Although delayed too long as far as I was concerned, the campus life at Emporia would get me out of the house. It would lead me to financial independence, and the final diploma would guarantee me the professional and intellectual respect due a school teacher.

Barely a week later, Mr. Fredrichs called: "Linda, can you be ready to leave on August 15 for freshman orientation? A room has opened up for first semester."

Could I ever! Mom, who was sorry to see me leave again but ecstatic that such an opportunity had plunked down in front of me, worked over my wardrobe that had just arrived from California. I would need new slacks and pullover sweaters, we agreed. And off we went, shopping at our old hangouts. Bypassing the sequined gowns I had once coveted, we headed straight for the racks of serviceable elastic-waist pants and coordinated tops. I could no longer consider the standard sizes of slacks; anything but "Talls" rode up my legs and left my ankles cold, to say nothing of unsightly.

Finally, when three sets fit both my tastes and my mother's, we went on to the shoe department. I ignored the high-fashion dress heels and concentrated on the practical, flat slip-on casuals which would make my life more comfortable.

When we left the store I felt as if I had left a part of my soul at the cash register, but I was equipped for wheelchair campus life. I was ready to do what had to be done.

Not a day too soon, Mom and I packed my trunk, and then I left. Mom had arranged transportation for me with our very dear, station-wagon-driving friend, Mary Fulmer. I was filled with as much hope as on the day I had flown to Aunt Bonnie's two years before.

As God closed one door, He opened a new one. I was eager to sing my private version of an old song: "We're rolling to Emporia."

6 Emporia, Hoorah!

Even today, the transition from sleep to consciousness transports me from the dreamy world of Emporia campus to real life in the suburbs. From one end to the other, the small college and cattle town was a handicapped person's paradise. I dance through those airy dreams as though the floor were cotton-candy clouds and I, weightless.

Physically, it seemed the best of all possible worlds, providing the security inherent in a large handicapped community, and the variety, stimulation, and camaraderie intrinsic to a college campus. Compared with living in the suburbs where hedges and front doors seem like foreboding barriers that separate neighbors from each other, cafeteria eating and sidewalk greeting made friend finding effortless.

For good or bad, one quick glance at the social make-up of the campus confirmed the existence of a nonregimented segregation: the handicapped ate and were friends with other handicapped; the blacks with other blacks; and white able-bodied with others like themselves. At the time I didn't mind. As I had clung to life in the hospital for no reason except that people there accepted me as I was, I relished the campus life for the physical security it wrapped around me. With these students, as confined as I, I was not the odd-one-out.

The advantage of the segregation was the comfort it provided. But, fortunately, the structure was not iron-clad, and I benefited from one of the exceptions to the unwritten rules: My best friend, that first year, was not disabled. Nina, one of my roommates, was the state-paid attendant of a third roommate, severely handicapped by cerebral palsy. Nina took notes for Suzie, helped her eat, dress, and get through the day. Nina, her boyfriend (also an attendant), and I became a fun-loving threesome—eating together, going to movies or plays, enjoying our hours not otherwise occupied with study or work.

Work was something I had determined not to be afraid of, and I would not quickly ask for assistance in doing anything I could feasibly do myself. I even changed my own linens, although with difficulty. I crawled around the bed on my hands and knees twice—first to take off the dirty set and once again to put on the clean. The job took up to a half-hour, but I finished with the satisfaction of knowing that I had done it without being a burden to anyone.

Busy. The word perfectly defines my Emporia days. I was once again consumed with life—to the point of ignoring my spiritual health.

The friends I made there were not Christians, and I was spiritually immature enough to allow them to play leader while I played follower. Did I not know how to maintain my growth as a Christian when I was separated from the friends who had led me to the Lord and held my hand for the first two years of my new life? Or did I just not care whether or not I made any progress on my journey toward the Celestial City?

Some of both, I'm sure.

My West-coast Christian friends were not replaced with new Christian friends. I'm ashamed to admit that I have never been one to keep up with long-distance correspondence, life in the here-and-now always having absorbed every iota of my attention and energy.

I attended the town's most obvious and convenient church for three years. Being adjacent to the campus, the church was as easy to get to as my classes. Its structure had no stairways to hurdle; its program had no convicting sermons to heed or ignore. I hardly noticed that the church people exuded little joy, only that I made few friends there. The fellow students I ran into were little different from most of the school's handicapped population: inwardly, if not outwardly, they directed an angry "why" to the God they thought smaller than their situations.

If I had looked harder, I could have found the spiritual encouragement I needed to keep me focused on the Word of God, but other things, like proving myself, were more important.

One of my distractions was forming a cheerleaders' group for the college's wheelchair basketball team. I would have been on the co-ed team if I could have conquered the dribbling and shooting, but cheerleading, less precise and more creative, suited me better. In itself it provided me with the exercise that was a healthy supplement to my daily doctor-prescribed regimen. Did we ever have fun—especially when the team played against able-bodied rivals, temporarily handicapped. Being unaccustomed to the rigors of dribbling with one hand while rolling a wheelchair with the other (no footwork allowed), the able-bodied team always lost, but they always provided us and the spectators with hilarious entertainment.

The urge to prove myself also raised its head in the classroom and library. This time I was not going to quit, and I was not going to be outdone. I wanted a degree, and I wanted it with honors. My tape recorder was my very present help in potential trouble. We made the grade together. After my first year, the dean's list was always lightened by my name.

In September of 1972 the mailman delivered another welcome surprise from the national headquarters of the MS Society—a "Would you be our guest?" invitation to the 1972 annual convention in Miami. The poster-girl campaign, for which I had posed—

MS strikes

the young

the strong

the beautiful—

had given me no official title or position. So attending an annual convention was not something I had thought my due right. However, I was delighted to be honored again as a representative of all MS patients. I would attend two workshops, emcee a luncheon, and be their guest at a banquet honoring Lorne Greene, the current chairman of the society. *Him I would like to meet,* I thought, anticipating shaking hands with the silver-haired giant of the Ponderosa, Ben Cartwright.

June Ingram, director of the Kansas chapter of the MS Society, was assigned as my traveling companion and Braniff, the carrier.

I had not been the target of so many cameras nor seen so many reporters since my beauty-queen days. The *Miami Herald* wanted to hear my comments on life the minute my feet touched the floor of the airport. The Associated Press wanted to interview me in my beach-front hotel room. "Good Morning, Miami" wanted me ready for live broadcast at 7:00 A.M. my first morning in town. That meant getting up at 5:30—a feat for me any day, but especially when I had gone to bed the night before tired enough to sleep for twenty-four hours straight.

Room service made eating breakfast simple enough, but it seemed we were the taxi driver's first customers—ever. Any other morning I might have enjoyed seeing all of Miami, but television cameras do not wait for lost cabbies. At 6:58 A.M. we arrived. We were ushered into the presence of smiling interviewers who fired questions, first at the medical doctor on the panel (*"What is MS?"*), then at me (*"What unique problems is a patient faced with?"*), then at the director of the national chapter (*"What services does the society provide patients?"*).

By the end of the half hour, I felt as if I had done a full day's work. The hot glaring lights pulled perspiration from my forehead until water beaded on my skin and dampened the roots of my hair. But who ever heard of a convention day's work being done by eight in the morning?

"Linda," warned June, "save some energy for the luncheon. There you'll really have to be on your toes."

The "Linda Light Luncheon"—I rolled past the easeled cardboard sign at the door of one of the hotel's many reception rooms. Earlier I had been prepped for my part by the national chairman, Daniel Haughton. "Each chapter will report its yearly fund-raising totals. All you have to do is introduce the chairperson of each chapter and give a plaque to the one who raised the most, which is

Linda as a toddler was a chubby pinup in her father's navy barracks in World War II; (below) At five, a fun-loving cowgirl.

A cheerleader at Capper Junior High in Topeka, Kansas; (below) With her father.

Two views of
Linda: in
swimsuit at
Miss Universe
competition,
and in eve-
ning gown
in earlier
Miss Kansas
pageant.

This was the promotional shot used to tout Miss Kansas for the Miss Universe competition; (below) A favorite family photo of the four Light daughters: Linda, Janet, Carole, Billie in front.

Linda as a TWA flight attendant; (above) sister Billie; (below) Linda and her mother, Winona Light, from whom Linda received her middle name.

Linda with actor Lorne Greene at the convention of the National Multiple Sclerosis Society in 1972; (above right) Linda's photo as the MS poster girl; (right) Ed and Eleanor Shumate, Linda's friends and counselors during college days.

Linda with the First Lady, Mrs. Patricia Nixon, honorary chairman of the MS fund drive in 1970; (right) Sister Janet and her daughter Nicole.

Del and Linda Strasheim

Linda and her sister Carole on Linda's wedding day, May 30, 1976; (below) Three generations of Nygrens: Patti; her mother Jerri, who also has MS; and Patti's niece Kristen.

New York." He handed me a set of cue cards and wished me well.

Actually, the luncheon was as boring as reading a telephone directory. *This could go on forever,* I thought when we were only halfway through the list. Finally, after the reports had droned on for several hours, I announced New York as the winner. As I leaned back from the microphone to lead the applause, a band of school-age children zoomed out from behind the curtained walls. They circled the large room on multicolored bicycles to the laughter and prolonged applause of the representatives of the chapters who had been outdone. Before disappearing behind the opaque drapes, their fearless leader approached and handed me a check for the amount of money they had raised in their Bike-a-thon.

I smiled gratefully: "Thank you *so* much for your hours of pedaling." Before I was able to elaborate, I looked down at the check: "Pay to the order of the Muscular Dystrophy Society."

Should I say nothing? Make a joke of it? I thought and spoke quickly: "I'm really sorry that Jerry Lewis couldn't be here to accept this check made out to the organization he sponsors, but I'm sure you all understand. . . ."

We all had a laugh at the mistake of some local volunteer who momentarily confused the two diseases, and then I dismissed us all to a free afternoon—to get ready for *the* banquet of the week.

I thought the afternoon off would mean a few hours of much-needed sleep, but once I was back in my room an old restlessness returned. I wanted a new dress. The one I had brought with me was surely adequate—but it wasn't new. When Nina had offered me the mint green, full-skirted gown, I had loved it. But I hadn't had a new formal in—

when I tried to think of how long it had been I only grew more depressed. Nothing short of a new dress would make me feel good about myself.

June and some of her friends who saw each other at every yearly convention had gone off to get a closer view of the sights we had passed on our around-the-town taxi ride, so I set off on my own to buy a memento of this Miami trip.

In the depths of the convention hotel, a row of boutiques leaned against one another. (I must not have been the only one who got this away-from-home buying urge.) I had hardly disembarked from the elevator before I had spotted the dress I wanted.

The bright paisley pattern seemed to pop right off the dark satin background. The cowl neck, empire waist, and A-line skirt fit the peppy mood I wanted to project as well as the season's fashion. The cut made me look—what shall I say—womanly. And the price? Well, I didn't splurge too often anymore. Before I laid my money on the counter, I saw Casey Howell, my southern California friend.

"Casey!" I hailed him.

Just the sight of him always lifted my spirits, and his stamp of approval on my selection finalized my decision.

I was glad I had taken the afternoon to spruce up. (A side-trip to the hairdresser's for a comb-out waylaid me on my journey back upstairs to my room for a rest that I never took.) I may have been tired by the time the gala started, but I felt more fashionable than I had in years.

I had assumed I would sit with the Kansas delegation, which included June and our local public-relations man, Hank. I had heard the seating arrangement would be somewhat structured—each state having its own designated area.

But, once inside the ballroom, I was informed of other, secret plans; Hank met me at the Kansas table with intentions of whooshing me away.

"Linda, we have a place reserved for you—at the head table." He pointed toward the platform raised several feet above the floor. Before I had time to protest, Hank and a stranger picked up my wheelchair and delivered me to the "for important people only" stage where I was greeted by the formidable Lorne Greene. He must have been used to awestruck women telling him they were fans of his, but I did it anyway, and he ate up every word of it as if it were the latest-breaking news story.

"Come and join us," he said, pointing to a seat next to my dinner companion, Louie Unser, a fellow patient and the brother of the race-car drivers, Al and Bobby.

Louie was a real card. If the evening had included only his lively conversation, I would have been content as a baby with a bottle of milk. His wit was sharp and his outlook drained of self-pity: "I just look at it this way: I'm on a permanent pit stop." Throughout the coming and going of the courses, we laughed until, like an alarm clock, I wound down.

The shift from our engaging dinner conversation to the evening's speeches was like the shift from forward to reverse. The program seemed as tedious as the afternoon's luncheon. When the formal presentations started, I allowed myself the luxury of thinking back over the years of my life. For a minute, which grew into five, then ten, I relived life as it had been ten years before, when I had first stepped foot in Miami as a Miss Universe contestant. Then I was strutting; now I was struggling. Then I was an empty-headed, selfish young girl with her sights set only on what she could get from the world; now I was a humbled young woman, uncertain as to whether she had anything left to give.

The city hadn't changed. The lights still dazzled (although this "light" was dim); the waves still lapped the beaches and mesmerized midwesterners. But what had become of my dreams? I generally tried to keep myself busy so that my mind didn't have time to wander off into the world where I imagined "What if—" or "If only—" until my carnal nature started singing the blues to itself. What if the crowds were still applauding my beauty? What if I—instead of Lorne Greene—were the talk of the ballroom?

Physically, but not emotionally, I was still in the red-walled banquet hall, watching the podium proceedings. I applauded Lorne's long speech. Then, with one ear, I realized some woman was being honored for the generosity of her contribution to the society.

How nice. But I wish they would hurry and get finished, I thought, before returning to my daydreams, which were suddenly interrupted. The national chairman's congratulatory remarks were punctuated, like a period, with "Linda Light," followed by the enthusiastic applause of four hundred sets of hands.

Did I wake up fast!

Daniel Haughton brought a fifteen-inch trophy-like cup to my seat, and someone set a microphone in front of me as if its presence alone were an instruction that I was to say something profound.

I hardly know what I'm being honored for, I thought. *Whatever . . .*

The applause died down and the audience that ringed the large tables waited for my thoughts, which I hadn't yet gathered. I was still in the tunnel of my mind's time machine, trying to catch up to the present celebration.

Emporia, Hoorah!

You've got to say thank you, I reasoned, but even that didn't come out well. I managed an impromptu two sentences: "I'm at a loss for words, but you know how very much I appreciate this. I don't think I can say any more or I'll cry—and then my mascara will run."

Nothing more needed to be said. No one would have heard it if I had tried. Without intending to be funny, I had brought the house down with much-needed laughter. (All of us had spent a week poring over a subject that had caused most of us to cry too many tears.)

And with my comment, the party started.

"Linda." Daniel spoke into the mike but addressed his last remarks to me: "Will you and Hank lead the evening's dancing?"

This announcement really took the cake. I didn't know what he was talking about. Dancing? Surely he meant some kind of symbolic "roll" out onto the dance floor. The music would start and Hank would twirl me and my chair around a few times before all the other gowned women were asked by their partners to gather around and show us how it's really done. I was game for whatever they had in mind. When Hank reached my side, I asked if he had any bright ideas about how we were going to do this.

"I'll take care of everything," he answered in a typically male just-leave-it-all-up-to-me tone of voice for which I was grateful.

With that, he rolled me to the dance floor, took hold of my arms, and lifted me up out of my chair. On cue, the orchestra played the first note of—I couldn't believe it—"Linda."

"Just lean against me, and I'll do all the work," Hank interrupted. By the time the second note of the song had traveled across the room, I was in tears. Was I laughing? Crying? I didn't know, but tears seemed the only appropriate expression for the surprise, the joy, the embarrassment (I didn't deserve all this attention), the delight of the moment.

I knew the words to the old World War II song, and so did Hank:

Whenever we meet,
My heart skips a beat,
I say to myself, "Hello, Linda" . . .

During the second time through the song, Hank whispered, "You're beautiful," into my ear.

For the moment, I believed him. His comment triggered the title of the song my California friends had introduced me to: "Something Beautiful." The lyrics seemed to fit the evening perfectly.

In a league far removed from the realm of Miss Universe, I was, for a day, the winner.

Beautiful.

How I wanted to believe that it would still be true the next morning, and the next, and the next.

Emporia,
Hoorah!

7 Will you Still Love Me Tomorrow?

For six months after the convention, I traveled to many U.S. cities, speaking to patients and raising funds. Keeping that schedule and keeping up with my studies wore me to a frazzle. The weeks have become another blur in my memory, except for the coming and going of Jack.

One evening in March my reading was interrupted by the dorm's intercom. "Linda?" the receptionist inquired.

I wheeled to the little metal box and assured her of my presence. "Yes?"

"You have a long-distance phone call."

The phone was halfway down the hall and when I got there, I discovered the voice on the other end was a stranger's. "Hello, Linda? This is Jack Bennett," he said. "You don't know me, but I saw you at the Miami convention. You and your story fascinated me, and I'd really like to meet you."

The request was the first of its kind, but it seemed sincere. "Oh?" I responded, wanting to hear more.

"I've had MS," Jack went on, "and I think my story might interest *you*. I've had a new treatment that has countered the MS—and I've recovered."

I was somewhat skeptical. MS is such a fickle disease that some patients' symptoms disappear for long periods of time. But it was commonly known that recovery was out of the question. "What do you mean?" I asked.

In a faraway southern drawl, he briefly described an experimental treatment that had worked for him: "Three years ago I was confined to a wheelchair. Now I'm walking. This is all because of a series of spinal injections that reversed the nerve damage. But I can't describe it all on the phone. I'd really like to come up next weekend and explain it further and let you see the results—firsthand."

"This weekend?" I happened to be free that Saturday.

"Sure. Would there be a motel where I could stay?"

"There's a Holiday Inn in town."

"If you would make me a reservation for Saturday night. . . . You can't believe how this treatment can change your life unless you see what it's done for me."

On a tentative note, we said good-by, and as the week progressed, my skepticism dissolved. If there was any possibility of my walking again, I wanted to know about it; I wanted to do it. By the time Jack arrived on Saturday, I was eager to listen to his story.

For four hours we sat in the Hornet's Nest, the snack shop in the student union, and talked. The management must have been relieved that Coke refills weren't on the house.

Once we had overstayed our welcome there, we went around campus, and, by late afternoon, I was convinced. Like a puppeteer, Jack had dangled a ticket to physical freedom in front of me. The doctors whose steroids had worked wonders for him would do the same for me. Throughout the day I watched him closely—no signs of MS, such as a raspy voice or flittering eyes. His slight limp seemed inconsequential compared to his former slavery to a wheelchair. The correlation was obvious: What was his could be mine.

The treatments would mean a trip to Birmingham, Alabama. The sooner, the better. The short hospital stay could be scheduled as soon as school was out in the spring. Jack, who seemed to have fallen in love with me before he set foot in Emporia, would pay all my expenses. I could stay with his parents before and after my admission. And once I was back on my feet . . .

That first weekend, the references to romance were vague, so vague I don't know whether or not he made them or I imagined them, but the daily letters that followed his return to Birmingham contained more and more talk of love and our future.

Promises. Although no one has ever learned a foolproof method for knowing what to believe and what to discount, I should have listened to Jack with more discerning ears and asked the advice of more mature people.

I sought the counsel of no one, not even God. My Bible? It was on my bookshelf—not packed away in my trunk—yet the concept of it being a "light unto my path" had escaped from me, as air slowly escapes through the knot in a once-full balloon.

Independence was still the name of the game. I told my family of my decision and trip only after the plans had been finalized. The plane ticket was in my hand; I was on my way to Birmingham.

Little did I know that God was masterminding a bigger plan than I could have imagined. On Saturday, March 30, a stranger could have been seen milling around campus, looking for someone he thought, but wasn't sure, he would recognize.

"Maybe I'll just run into her on the sidewalk," he hoped, dreading the awkwardness of a formal introduction and meeting.

But I wasn't cruising the sidewalks that day. I was out of town on one of my speaking engagements.

That solo reconnaissance of the casually dressed thirty-one-year-old man proved futile. He would have to find help in locating me. The student directory in the campus's most visible dorm complex, Twin Towers, only complicated matters. Linda Light was listed twice and lived in two different buildings. The knot that had been growing in his stomach started to shrink, only because it was being pulled taut and settling in for a good, long stay.

He turned the book around and pointed to the two listings, so that the woman behind the desk could interpret his double vision.

She laughed. "Do you want the one in the wheelchair?"

Del was relieved to know the distinction would be so easily made, and he set off in the direction of my dorm, Morse Hall. To get there, he had to cross the bridge over the lake. By the time he reached the far side, his nerve had failed him. "I'll just walk around the building once before I go in," he thought.

Around once. Twice. Three times. "This has to stop. People will be looking out their windows and wondering if my name is Joshua."

If he were going to make it inside the front doors of the dorm, he knew he was going to need help, and his faith in his silent, unseen partner set his thoughts heavenward: "Lord," he sighed, "give me the strength I need to walk through that doorway," and, after taking a deep breath, he made it.

Hesitantly, he walked up to the receptionist and said, "Linda Light, please."

She spoke into the switchboard's microphone and received no answer.

"I'm sorry, she's not here," she replied. A slight nod of her head and an "I'm sorry" in her eyes told Del what he needed to know.

"Oh, that's okay," he said as if my absence really were something she might be responsible for. "It's okay," he reassured her. "I'll come back another time."

Despite his seemingly useless five-hundred-mile round-trip drive, he was ecstatic. Just getting to the lobby of my dorm and establishing where I was seemed victory enough for one day.

"May I leave this for her?" he asked, sliding across the desk a sealed envelope and a small gift-wrapped package. And with that he was gone, back into hiding in Nebraska.

When I returned home that evening, I opened the package containing the potholder his mother had made and read his note:

Dear Linda,

I have read a lot about you and find you an inspiration.

I am a thirty-one-year-old bachelor from Nebraska and would like to meet you someday. If you care to correspond, my address is enclosed.

Sincerely,
Del Strasheim

"That's cute," I thought and then went on with my nightly bedtime routine. Within minutes my mind was back on Jack and my future in Alabama.

Too bad for Del Strasheim that I'm not available for "getting to know" any eligible bachelors.

Jack and his parents, all smiles, met me at the Birmingham airport and drove me to their Tara-style mansion. The older couple looked the part of the genteel landowners they were, and they graciously hosted my visit. After all, could I be their future daughter-in-law?

Jack lived nearby and came to his parents' home for all his meals. Then, and in the private hours in between, I dreamily delighted in his attentions. He filled my ears with plans: "When you're back on your feet, you can move down here. Then we'll—" The list of what we would do together lengthened by the hour.

Once on my feet—the words were like museum jewels, prized beyond price. I would run around the campus. I would do the splits in front of the cheering fans. I would take on stairs three at a time. And yes, I would, for the love of a man, move to Alabama.

Even during this week when we basked in each other's presence, I think he never said the word *marriage.* But the word's absence was overshadowed by the prevalence of his kisses and the desperation with which I received them. Right there, in my arms, was the man who had, intermittently since my release from the hospital, been the object of my dreams. He wanted me. He told me I was beautiful. Surely those frequently repeated lines meant that he intended to take care of me, in sickness and in health until one of us died. His assurances that I would be able to walk again reminded me of my potential; I could be as desirable as I once had been.

When I had been able to choose, by winking, any dance partner in a room, I had known the difference between attentions and intentions. (Can it be only coincidental that the sound and spelling of the two words are so similar?) Hadn't I had enough sense to ignore Ben's talk of marriage until he had pulled a diamond ring from his pocket? What had happened to me? I was so starved for attention that I would lunge at any able-bodied male who gave it to me. (It just so happened that Jack was good looking.) It is the trap into which so many handicapped women walk.

On one level, who can fault them?

I remember as clearly as if it were yesterday, Carole taking me in my wheelchair to an airport check-in counter. The male attendant quickly glanced at the two of us. Although it was obvious that I, not Carole, was the passenger, he refused to acknowledge me as such or talk to me. Looking straight at Carole he asked, "Where is she going?" and "Where would she like to sit?" as though I were a child too young to take care of myself. The ticket counter that separated the attendant from me shielded him from the bite of the frost that proceeded from my mouth.

I was not about to let any male treat me as a nonperson. My reaction was inexcusable. The pattern of men turning, even if ever-so-slightly, from me rather than treating me like an adult, to say nothing of an attractive woman, had worn me down to the point where I believed vague words and warm kisses represented a love maybe not bigger than God's but surely as long-lasting and more tangible.

And the more I believed, the more I believed.

The spinal injections were given while I was drugged but not unconscious. The operating room was a blur of green gowns, only momentarily interrupted by a shattering twinge of pain. It seemed easy enough. The first of four injections

*Will You
Still
Love Me
Tomorrow?*

125

was over. Within minutes the green gowns rolled me back to my hospital room where I slept until the next morning, when I awoke expectantly.

Being a quarter of the way through the treatment, I thought I should be a quarter better than twenty-four hours before. I swished my arms and legs against the sanitized bedsheets and decided it was time to see myself to the rest room.

I sat up, dangled my feet from the bed and slid off the side. But I got no further. An explosion went off in my head.

I fell onto the bed not because of my weak knees but because the pain in my temple made any other action impossible. There I lay, muffling my moans with a blanket until the nurse put me properly to bed. A few minutes later, I threw up at the sight of a tray full of food set before me by a young aide.

When the doctor arrived at my side, he looked puzzled. With a small metal hammer he gave me a few taps, immediately followed by a few "H'ms" but no clear words.

The pain was subsiding, but the general feeling of malaise was constant. I was sick, as if I had some incapacitating flu, and I wanted him to do something about it.

"Let's see how you are in the morning," he replied noncommittally yet compassionately.

He left without doing anything, and I wandered in and out of a restless sleep until Jack bounded into my room, eager for some show of newly acquired agility. His caramel-colored hair was windblown, and he was slightly out of breath.

"How's my lady?" he asked, his green eyes wide with anticipation.

"Oh, hi," I answered groggily.

This was not what he had expected. The treatments had prompted immediate improvement for him. By this time, according to his—and my—

calculations, we should have been planning a celebration party.

I didn't take my head off the pillow. For the duration of his short stay, I hardly spoke except for yes or no, as if I were on the receiving end of his Twenty Questions. His visit tired me. The more listless I grew, the more restless he grew, until he announced he had to leave. His "good night" included a whisper in my ear: "Be patient. It may not take effect for another day."

As I returned to the land of sleep, my mind whirled with thoughts of waiting, but nothing I would describe as patience. *I want this "flu" to leave. I want to be able to eat. I want to be well.* But those thoughts were bulldozed to the forefront by bigger demands: *I want to walk. When is the magic going to work?*

For five days the gray-haired, gentle doctor said next to nothing. For five days Jack came to visit, each time a little more apprehensive, a little less enthusiastic about what the next day would bring.

Gradually my internal questions grew monstrous. *Are there going to be more treatments? When are we going to get on with this? When is someone going to come and save me?*

The answers arrived on the sixth morning. I awoke from a nap to the sight of Harold and Rachel, Jack's mother and father, smiling somewhat nervously. The doctor had arranged his plans with them. "He recommends you go to a hospital in Memphis, Tennessee, to recuperate," said Rachel.

I didn't know what she meant by that word. "Recuperate from what?" Doctors had never done well by me, and five days of noncommittal hemming and hawing had made me more than a little wary. "Am I worse off now than I was before?"

"You were a very unusual case," Rachel said in a

most reassuring tone, "and you had an adverse reaction to the steroid. It will just take time."

"Time—for what?"

"Time for you to feel like your normal self again."

Normal, I knew, was a relative term. "Normal—like two weeks ago?" I asked, afraid I already knew the answer. It had been a long time since anyone had said anything about walking.

"Linda—" Rachel tried to soften the impact of the news: the injection hadn't and wouldn't affect my MS. I wouldn't walk again. Recuperation was the word used for my journey out of bed and back into my wheelchair.

"Here," Rachel continued, "I'll help you dress, and Harold will take care of your discharge papers. Then we'll be off to Memphis. We've put a mattress in the back of the station wagon. I think you'll be comfortable there."

The life had been knocked out of me. My physical weakness and new hopelessness returned me to my state-hospital mindset. They probably could have said they were driving me to Alaska. I wouldn't have balked. To a northerner, Memphis and Birmingham may sound far apart, but they are really neighboring cities. The drive took only four hours.

As Rachel packed my bags, she kept a steady stream of conversation flowing, not once mentioning Jack. I didn't think it unusual, but just assumed he must have stayed in the car, wanting to keep the commotion of my leaving to a minimum. It was probably just as well, I thought. Rachel, who had outdone herself in making me feel welcome and at ease with her, was, in motherly fashion, taking control. Another person might have been underfoot, and besides, this way I had a few extra minutes to compose myself before seeing him.

Surely he would have felt the blow of my disappointment. He was saving his comfort for the ride.

But when we reached the car, the doors were locked and the seats empty. No Jack sat inside perusing the newspaper.

"Will we be picking up Jack?" I ventured, pushing from my mind an image that flashed through it. For an instant I had been sitting in my parents' living room when my father had locked himself from the sight of me.

Before Rachel answered my question, another image sped through: Ben and Mom walking out of the state hospital as the orderlies were grabbing my arms.

"He won't be going with us," Rachel said apologetically.

And without her saying anything more, I knew what had happened.

Abandoned. It was the nightmare of my life.

Why? why? why? I demanded.

My system shifted into overload, and everything blurred for about a week.

Plans? I was nowhere. How had I got myself into this mess? Why had I believed empty promises? Jack was gone, never again within my reach or even sight. Why hadn't I seen that he hadn't loved me—just as I was? That his love had always been connected to "when you're back on your feet"? Men? They were all alike. Full of ulterior motives I didn't understand and didn't want to understand. I hated them. My father? He was a man. And Jack's rejection of me compounded my resentments toward him who had first "left" me. God? If He was in control, He had a pretty sick sense of humor.

Hope returned briefly when the neurological staff felt that there was a very good chance that I had a brain tumor. The possibility that there *was* a tumor, *maybe* operable . . . But negative results to the painful, intricate tests once again drained my hopes.

For weeks I lay in a Memphis bed and steamed—right below the boiling point. I could have out-scowled and out-cried any of the bitter Emporia students or any of my fellow hospital patients. The i.v. bottle that dripped over my head may as well have been leaking burning acid into my veins.

One evening, just as the sun was setting, I boiled over. There was a limit to the length of time my anger at God—at everyone—could simmer. I had held it in long enough. As if God didn't already know what was consuming me, I let Him have it.

Being angry that God was even behind the setting of the sun and the coming of another darkness, I directed my audible accusations to the half of the fiery ball I could still see above the skyline.

I had memorized a few Scripture promises in California. I flung 1 Corinthians 10:13 in God's face: "God is faithful; he will not let you be tempted beyond what you can bear."

"I trusted you and you lied to me," I charged. "You *have* given me more than I can bear." My fury released a torrent of tears. (I had thought the last few weeks had drained the cistern.) The sobbing didn't subside until my physical strength simply gave out.

That night God came through with no audible answers. He churned no windstorm, zapped no lightning, nor did He send by any chaplain the next morning to pray for me.

But neither had He, as I then thought, reneged on His promise.

I've since learned that the farther *we* walk from Jesus, the less we feel that He loves us. Only hindsight showed me that He had not left me totally friendless, for Rachel, like an angel of mercy sent to hold my hand, stayed in Memphis with me the entire summer. Where would I have been without her and without the *daily* fresh rose delivered to my bedside out of the generosity of the doctor whose miracle treatment hadn't worked? Who but an angel would have slept for six weeks on a fold-away cot in someone else's hospital room and spent six weeks' worth of days smiling, reading, and gift giving to a sick woman she had just recently met? The hand of God was faithful, despite my wandering years and rebellious declaration of independence.

Maybe Rachel felt guilty for her son's disappearance. Maybe the doctor felt guilty for my long confinement. No matter what their motives were, they were Godsends in a weary land, and they saw me through to the end of the ordeal. Rachel even escorted me back to Kansas City where I was greeted by my sister Janet and her new husband.

Isn't it a wonder? God never forgets His own. "If we are faithless, he will remain faithful, for he cannot disown himself" (2 Timothy 2:13).

In September I returned to school, but not without the persuasion of a Memphis hospital psychiatrist who knew that reestablishing some plans and goals would force me toward recovery.

Less than enthusiastically, I rolled back into the dormitory I had thought I might never reenter, surely never on wheels. But little did I know what (or whom) the school year would bring through the same doorway—the tender mercy God had been molding for me for thirty-two whole years.

8 Open my Ears That I May Hear

During my Emporia days, people entered my life via the metal intercom box attached to the wall in my room and wired to the front-desk switchboard.

The "Linda" that broke into the silence of my studies pumped anticipation through my bloodstream. Who was wanting to tell me what?

Although calls came frequently, the one I waited for was never dialed into Ma Bell's system. Topeka may as well have been on another continent; Mom or Dad never asked to hear my voice. Mom's excuse was logical, but slightly lame: "Dad says we just can't afford long-distance phone bills." That's what she said. I heard: "Dad says that money is more important than you are," and I simply didn't want to hear it.

Occasionally, I called them. When I was paying, Mom was all ears. I was all gab, filling her in on all the good days and skimming over the bad. Then I would switch gears and ask her about herself. "Fine. Fine," she would clip and then she would go on about Billie's school adventures, making precious few references to Dad or even to herself.

The one time I tried to reach around the screen that continued to separate Dad from me, I felt beaten away not by words but by the silence to which I should have grown accustomed but hadn't.

My third school year had gone well. In temporal ways my determination had paid off: *Who's Who Among Students in American Universities and Colleges* had deemed me worthy of its 1973 roster. It may seem no honor compared to having tea with the first lady or receiving a fifteen-inch trophy from the National MS Society, but in my book this was the top of the mountain. I had proven Father wrong; I had won the race.

"Hello, Dad, this is Linda," I called home to tell him about my "gold medal" award. I had been hoping Dad would pick up the receiver. I wanted to hear his "well done."

"Guess what?" I continued.

He couldn't guess.

"I made *Who's Who*." I knew he had heard of the award and I didn't further explain its importance.

I may as well have said I had dialed the phone myself. (There had been times when that had been difficult for me!)

He grunted.

"*Who's Who in American Universities and Colleges.*" *I'll just remind him of what it is.* "It's a national honor given to only the all-around top students in the country. I'm only one of four chosen from here at Emporia."

"So, what else is new?"

I didn't have the strength to force out of him the acknowledgment I needed to hear. The hours preceding this call had been filled with daydreams of father rolling me across the stage to pick up the certificate, then taking me back to my place at the left of the podium and, just before sitting down next to me, leaning over and whispering the words that would erase the pain: "Good work, kid."

But no. The dreams were what was erased. I knew I would ask June Ingram to be my surrogate parent. Mom would say that Dad needed her to be at home and that she was sorry she couldn't come.

I hung up the phone and dragged back to my room and my studies, hoping someone would call to cheer me up.

As I was leaving my room one Saturday afternoon in early April of 1974, the voice from the metal box on the wall called me back. The door I was locking blocked me from the microphone through which I could respond. I didn't know why I didn't ignore the summons. I was late for a matinee; my date was waiting for me at the side entrance of the dorm.

Maybe Phil has been held up, I thought as I fussed with the keys. I found that just ignoring the intercom was impossible. My curiosity had a way of getting the best of me. Any call *could* be too important to miss.

"Yes," I answered after the second page had sliced the silence.

"You have a visitor."

"Who is it?" I inquired somewhat impatiently. "I'm not expecting anyone. I'm on my way out. . . ." My voice trailed off.

A long pause followed. I knew she was relaying my question to the caller who stood across the desk from her.

"Del Strasheim. He says that if you're busy, he'll come back another time."

"All right by me."

The guy from Nebraska. I clearly remembered his name, even though it had been a full year since he had left his mysterious note. *Why would anyone take twelve months to return a call?* I wondered. *Probably the spring air,* and with that, I again dismissed him from my mind. I went off on my date, relieved that the call had not interrupted my afternoon plans.

Now Del tells me he doesn't know what made him return the very next weekend, except, of course, the inner tug of the Holy Spirit. (Maybe He works overtime in the spring.) Maybe Del thought he had to come once for each time he had seen my picture. In three and a half years, the *Parade* story had never (well, hardly ever) left his wallet. But because of my trip to Miami an Associated Press wire photo of me found its way into a corner of the local newspaper he skimmed each morning before heading to the office where he worked as an architect. When he had seen the photo, Del gulped his coffee and read every letter of the fine print. He had thought I was still living in California, not, as the story said, right next door in Kansas.

His third sighting of my name in print can be nothing short of a miracle. Once a month Del spent an evening in the public library, perusing the magazines that covered one wall. *Time. Newsweek. Reader's Digest.* I can understand him skimming those general readership magazines, but *Today's Health?* A magazine geared to the medical profession? Shortly after my appearance in Miami, *Today's Health* also had run a story, a blend of facts on MS and the personal-interest feature on my reaction to the disease. That third sighting prompted him to make his first, ill-fated trip, and now, a year later, he walked into my line of vision for real.

The encounter was brief. Wouldn't you know, he woke me from a nap. With rumpled clothes and one side of my hair rebelliously flattened against my head (I did run a comb through it, but to no avail), I slowly paddled down the long hall to the lounge.

The sleep hadn't left my head. *This character better be worth the trouble he's causing,* I thought. Little did I know that I would ever value any man as highly as I would one day value this one.

The only stranger in the room smiled in my direction. As if smiling were contagious, I returned the greeting before saying hello. Behind his dark-rimmed glasses his brown eyes tried to hide. His face flushed at the sight of me, and he didn't, except for a fleeting second, look straight into my eyes. His nervousness was as obvious as my handicap.

"Are you Del?" I asked. The question seemed obvious but necessary.

He looked directly at my lips. "Yes. Linda?" He held out his hand for me to shake as if he were making a business acquaintance.

What next? I wondered. Clearly he was uncomfortable and I wanted to put him at ease as soon as I could. "Shall we find you a seat?" I asked, pointing to the chairs circling the room. Maybe he would feel better if he were down on my level.

"Sure," and he walked at my side to an upholstered armchair next to which I pulled up my wheelchair.

Although the lengthy *Today's Health* article had not actually said I was a Christian, Del had read between the lines: "Linda is a child of God." And that hunch prompted his first request: "My mom and I read about you, and we both find your story so interesting. She gets depressed so easily and can be bitter at times. I thought if you could write out your testimony for her, it would help her. Just a few lines of encouragement would lift her spirits."

I knew enough about depression that I wanted

to help anyone wage war against it. But he seemed to be asking for a testimony to my faith in God. Could I write a sincere statement of my confidence in Him when I had so recently lashed out and accused Him of forsaking me?

When confronted with this stranger's request, a faith stirred deep inside me as if it were waking from hibernation. I did believe or at least desired to believe that God was sovereign and working to bring about His good. Yes, I *could* claim His promises for Del's mother.

"Of course, I'll write her a note," I replied.

From his inner coat pocket he pulled a piece of paper and a pen that he apparently had brought specifically for this purpose. Without another word, he handed them to me. This silent gesture was a second way of asking his request.

Suddenly I panicked. "I spoke too fast," I said, somewhat embarrassed. "I didn't know you meant for me to do it here and now. Writing with a pen or pencil is a problem for me."

His face warmed with compassion, nudging me to risk his impatience on a judgmental glance. "But I'll get a few sentences out, if you're patient enough."

He looked as if he would have waited till the sun burned out.

Slowly I scrawled:

Your son is here visiting me today, and he asked that I write a note of encouragement to you. My life has been full of many trials, but my trust in God and faith in His Son has kept me going. He has carried me through many deep valleys, and I could not go on without Him. I know this note is brief, but my hand gets cramps if I write too long.

Sincerely,
Linda Light

I looked up into his face that was as gentle-looking as a lamb's. He relieved my hands of their load, said, "Thank you," and then, instead of making further conversation, asked his second request: "May I come back again?"

His smile. There was something boyishly innocent and irresistible about it.

"Sure," I flashed my best camera-ready grin back at him, and he was gone.

I made my way back to my room. *Why didn't he stay and talk?* I wondered even though I had a hunch why he left so quickly. My years at Emporia had sensitized me to people's handicaps. As he had been ready to leave I had realized that his eyes glanced toward my lips every time I spoke. It hadn't been mentioned, but he obviously had a hearing problem, to which I didn't give a second thought. In this community who didn't have a physical impairment? *That may have been why he didn't linger, but he should have known. . . .* With that unfinished thought in my head, I went back to sleep. When I woke for dinner, Del's coming and going seemed like a pleasant dream: A handsome brown-haired man had entered the scene and immediately put me at ease. He hadn't shown evidence of harboring preconceived ideas of who I should be or how I should respond. He hadn't seen me as a woman with whom he might play games (no "macho-man" airs). He had looked at me through pure eyes. To him I had been an individual of worth—nothing more, nothing less.

Three days later the mailbox contained concrete proof. My Saturday afternoon sleep *had* been interrupted.

A letter from Del detailed the effect of my short testimony on his mother:

> Much to my surprise, when I returned home from seeing you, I discovered that my mom and two sisters were at my apartment. They'd come to town

for a day of shopping and had stopped by my place to say hello.

As they were heading toward their car to leave, I asked Mom if she would come back into the apartment for a minute, and then I handed her your note.

Linda, your encouragement moved her to tears. She was deeply moved that I would have found you and that you would have taken the time to share with her.

Thank you again for your interest. I know it has turned Mom's face toward the Lord.

Sincerely,
Del Strasheim

I meant to respond—I really did. But God only knows what happened to the envelope of Del's letter containing the return address. I was glad that I had been of help and found myself slightly encouraged that such a man existed. But I chalked up my encounter with him as a fluke opportunity to influence someone into the kingdom and gave him little thought until he again arrived at my door three months later, just before summer break.

Del, who had interpreted my silence as disinterest, even rejection, nearly never returned. He had nerve enough to drive the two hundred and fifty miles and then stopped. Driving toward and then onto campus was one thing. Getting out of his car and walking toward the dorm was quite another. He sat in the parking lot outside Morse Hall, empty of courage, full of questions, all of which boiled down to one: *Why am I here?*

Del, who was more accustomed than I to talking over every detail of his life with his heavenly Father, thought maybe there had been a break in the communication between the two of them. Del *had* been sure the Lord was behind his fourth trip, which was not prompted by his mother's moods. He had been praying (oh, how he had been praying) that God would alleviate his loneliness. Hadn't God placed me in his path—or at least on his mind and not far from his path? And hadn't Del been faithful in pursuing the Spirit-planted desire?

So what was the problem? Why was his nerve as absent as it had been every other time he had ever sought out the company of a woman?

In the seclusion of his Pontiac, Del's questions were interrupted by the flight of a yellow-breasted bird whose dive from a nearby evergreen crossed within inches of Del's windshield. The spray of color reminded him of a familiar promise: "Look at the birds of the air; they do not sow or reap or store away in barns, and yet your heavenly Father feeds them. Are you not much more valuable than they?" (Matthew 6:26).

Like a skywriter, the bright bird had left a message. Del breathed in the gift of courage and breathed out a "Thank You, Lord." He was ready for another conversation with the switchboard operator and with me.

That balmy afternoon I was prepared for visitors. I answered his summons wearing a cheery sombrero and a pair of sporty shorts that revealed just enough of my presummer tan to make me feel rewarded for my sunbathing efforts.

"Hello! How are you?" I greeted him as I approached.

"Fine, and you?"

Before I answered even his first question, I wanted to know if I was making myself clear to him. "Am I speaking loud enough for you?"

As he assured me he could understand me, I was astonished at the muddiness of his speech; it had thoroughly escaped me during our first meeting. (Could I have been that sleepy?)

Inwardly I smiled at my own deafness; he spoke hardly three more sentences before my ears were opened. I heard a whole new voice—one as imperfect in enunciation as mine was in tone. No wonder he had, at our first meeting, been a man of so few words.

We settled into the same corner of the large room as we had before, and Del continued our getting-to-know-you conversation by handing me the brown-wrapped package he clutched under his left arm.

"This is no potholder," I laughed as I slipped my fingers under the Scotch tape and unveiled the back side of a framed canvas. The paper fell to the floor and I flipped the painting over to get a glimpse of the real surprise.

"Oh my—y—y—y," I exclaimed at the sight of the bright oranges and golds of a painting of two of nature's most impressive wonders: The sky was ablaze with a fiery sunset and twice pierced with majestic twin Rock spires.

"I've called it 'Rock Towers,'" explained Del, as self-conscious as a painter who didn't know whether or not he was good.

"*You* did this?" His face flushed even redder than when he had first met me. "It's wonderful. You have such an eye—or is it in the hands? Now, if I were to try something like this—"

We both laughed and then enjoyed an afternoon as pleasant as any I can remember. I played tour guide, showing him the campus and the town whose brick houses were scaled by full-bloomed rose bushes.

That evening, his "good night" lingered in my ears but not on my lips, which his didn't touch. But the absence of his kiss didn't even cross my mind, and I thought of him as the brother I had never had. The afternoon stroll had filled my expectations.

Bless his heart, Del was the most persistent yet indirect suitor the world has ever seen. Maybe I had learned my let-the-vulnerable-beware lesson too well and forbidden myself to read between the lines of any man's prose. I liked him; I liked his gentle, unassuming manner, but romance or wedding bells were as far from my mind as retirement is to a twenty-five-year-old.

At the end of the school year I told him I was going to Carole's for the summer. He wrote me there, but did I answer?

From September to June I had run on nervous energy. When I sat down in Carole's yard to catch my breath, I collapsed, too exhausted and sick with a bladder infection to answer my mail.

Despite the stab of rejection Del suffered every day when he saw no "Light" in his mailbox, he returned to Emporia in the fall, confident that God wanted him to pursue a friendship with me.

And that semester I found out more about who he was. He could hear 40 percent of what most of us can. No doctor had been there to confirm the cause or immediate effect, but it seemed the culprit had been a 1945 measles epidemic. When the rash had disappeared, his older brother and youngest sister couldn't hear anything. Del had fared a little better than they.

He didn't have a hearing aid because the static emitted from it produced an earache. He and I communicated best by typewriter; he would pull up a chair next to mine and we would peck away, sentence after slow sentence.

I could not figure out how Del had learned the intricacies of his profession. Thank God for the printed word. Would Del have otherwise learned his trade—or heard the good news of salvation? In January of 1970, just months before seeing the feature in *Parade*, he accepted Christ through the influence of a tract given him by his brother Don, and four years of in-depth study of the Scripture had left its mark. Del's return trips revealed his wealth of spiritual knowledge and the depth to which the roots had grown and taken hold.

One Saturday, early in that school year, Del felt particularly adventurous and wheeled me around to the wrong side of his car. "Want to drive?" he asked, offering to take his life into his own hands.

I fiercely shook my head *no,* but kept a glint in my eye that said "I can be convinced."

"You want to?" Del repeated. "We'll go down to the auxiliary parking lot and give it a whirl."

I said neither *yes* nor *no,* but let him drive to the lot on the far edge of campus. It was nearly empty since many of the car owners had returned to their home towns for the weekend.

"Okay?" he asked again, encouraging me by squeezing my hand and making his big calf eyes shout, "Go ahead. Drive it."

With delight I remembered that first drive around the block when I was twelve. Maybe I could, for a few minutes, recapture the exhilarating independence.

"Let's switch places," I motioned, and, within thirty seconds, there I sat behind the wheel of his 1970 Pontiac, ready to turn on the ignition.

Del, as excited as I was, patiently looked on but did not interfere with my meanderings. We let ourselves pretend that my perception was as perfect as Al Unser's.

I started our "trip" cautiously, not venturing over ten miles per hour.

"Give it more gas," Del encouraged. I suddenly forgot all my inhibitions and let it go as fast as I dared—from one end of the lot to the other, circle after imperfect circle—I certainly, and the tires nearly, squealing all the way.

Even after I came to a stop and turned off the

ignition, my inner motor kept racing. I turned to Del who applauded my efforts with laughter and a daring, brotherly "I love you" hug that spoke louder than words.

Del's love was a curiosity to me. Behind the walls of silence, God had chiseled out the most wonderful, most loving creation I could imagine. If I were to have compared the fruit of the Spirit—love, joy, peace, patience, kindness, goodness, faithfulness, gentleness, and self-control—manifested in my life with those in Del's, I would have placed myself at sea level and Del on top of Pike's Peak.

Whereas he, like Jesus as described in Hebrews 12, seemed to have learned obedience from the things he had suffered, I needed to be taken by the hand and escorted into the knowledge of the Lord.

What was unconditional love like? Reading about it in the Gospels was one thing, but receiving it from a flesh and blood man was something else—and unsettling.

I couldn't imagine the eyes of any of the men I had previously known brimming with delight over my weaving a car around an empty parking lot. They would have been full of disdain or pity. If I had then known how many nights Del eventually would get out of bed and hold my head and stroke my hair as some flu or sheer exhaustion prompted me to lose the dinner I had eaten a few hours earlier, I might have run away from him. I would have been afraid for him to get a bull's-eye view of my mortality, in much the same way as Eve, embarrassed of her sin, tried to hide herself from God.

But my trust grew a little at a time, slower than a bud grows into a flower.

That day—the day he allowed me the freedom to be myself despite my shortcomings—gave me my first glimpse into the Ephesians 5 definition of Christ's perfect love for His bride, the church. I didn't then think about God's corresponding mysterious design for marriage: a husband and wife being an earthly model of Christ's relationship with humanity, but the apostle Paul perfectly explained the union toward which Del and I were heading:

> The husband is the head of the wife as Christ is the head of the church, his body, of which he is the Savior. Now as the church submits to Christ, so also wives should submit to their husbands in everything.
>
> Husbands, love your wives, just as Christ loved the church and gave himself up for her to make her holy, cleansing her by the washing with water through the word, and to present her to himself as a radiant church, without stain or wrinkle or any other blemish, but holy and blameless. In this same way, husbands ought to love their wives as their own bodies. He who loves his wife loves himself. After all, no one ever hated his own body, but he feeds and cares for it, just as Christ does the church—for we are members of his body. "For this reason a man will leave his father and mother and will be united to his wife, and the two will become one flesh." This is a profound mystery—but I am talking about Christ and the church. However, each one of you also must love his wife as he loves himself, and the wife must respect her husband. (Ephesians 5:23–33)

Christmas. I think the magic of the day is the hope that is wrapped inside each gift—from the best gift of all, the Christ child, to the tiniest gift-wrapped box or the least-ornamented card. Behind or inside the presents I see the presence and the love of the giver—and love always promises hope.

Christmas 1975—that season God opened the gates of heaven and poured out a bundle of gifts that was bigger than all the bundles thrown over every Santa's shoulder: He nudged a classmate who was a dedicated Christian to invite me to her home, just six blocks from campus, for the holidays.

Inside the walls of the Shumates' home, I was surrounded by God's love in action for the first time in my life. My new friend Jeri and her parents, Eleanor and Ed (whom I loved to call "Oedipus the King"), adopted me—not only for the duration of the vacation but for the rest of my single life.

After I had soaked up a few days' worth of the Christian atmosphere that pervaded the air of their home like Christmas carols that float from stereo speakers, Eleanor summed up her prescription for my spiritual health: "What you need is a bath of Christian fellowship," and I knew she was right.

The longer I stayed at Emporia, the less I saw the place through rose-colored glasses. By this time, my fourth full year, I defined the moral environment in terms of Sodom and Gommorah. I never knew what or whom (and in what array or lack of it) to expect in the dorms or even in the open air of the campus. The smell of incense and marijuana escaped from under closed doors and permeated hallways. Mother had taught me a long list of things that nice girls didn't do. I may have wandered from the straight and narrow, but my conscience kept to a relatively tight budget.

I was simply tired of proving myself scholastically, socially, *and* waging a personal battle in the dorm: The first semester of that year had set me down in the worst rooming situation of my college career. My two roommates fought like tomcats. And I was caught in the middle. Even when they weren't at each other's throats, they, individually, were a drain on me. One of them had spent several years on the fringes of a fanatical religious group, and nearly every night her sleep was punctuated with tormenting nightmares. She may have slept through them, but I didn't. Her desperate cries for Jesus' help sent my head under the thick insulation of my foam pillow. Her shouts sounded as if they were coming from the brink of hell, as if she were on the edge of the precipice and calling for deliverance from the lapping flames.

The other woman was a fervent member of one of the major religious cults who saw me as a pagan who was needlessly suffering. Between the two of them, my requirement for Valium had increased almost weekly.

The Shumates' extended invitation was half of my Christmas love and hope.

The second half I viewed as such only with hindsight.

It was delivered by the Postal service and looked like a card—until it was opened. It was from Del. As I tore open the flap, I was pleased that he had thought of me by sending a card.

The stationery inside matched the burnished yellow envelope. *Not really very Christmasy,* I noted, before starting to read the perfectly aligned script that looked like a professionally printed invitation.

I don't know what I would have done if I had read the last line first. Even the opening paragraph was more forthright than Del had previously been:

> *Dear Linda,*
>
> *that day I first met you*
> *caused my heart to rise*
> *on a day that was so blue*
> *you were a pleasant surprise*
>
> *life can be so sweet*
> *knowing someone like you*

often when I am down and beat
your friendship lifts my blues

spring is always near
when life's burdens wear us low
April showers begin to appear
bringing flowers and rainbows

spring, when earth awakens
and fading hopes are revived
flower garden paths beckon
and our paths, Jesus guides

many nights I have not slept
for many sorrows I quietly bear
but the Scriptures say Jesus wept
and therefore I know He cares

much have you meant to me
with your gentleness
my burdens seem wee
because of your kindness

I prayed to the Lord nightly
to help make this friendship grow
He never takes my prayers lightly
for I feel this friendship glows

but I keep praying further
asking for something dear to me
and I often do wonder
what is His will for me

my heart must be opened
for, weary does it grow by day
to hold back, unspoken
what it aches to say

please, answer my wondering
let me know His will for me
I love you and care enough to be asking
Linda, will you marry me?

I took a deep breath and started back at the beginning. "Oh, my," I said aloud to myself. For a few moments I had no clear thoughts, only confused feelings. Then questions mounted up: *What is he talking about? Doesn't he see that we don't know each other well enough?* (I *liked* him and was comfortable with him, but, since my trip to Alabama, marriage had seemed unthinkable.) *Doesn't he see that I can't be a good wife in this condition? Doesn't he see that it's an impossibility. (Hadn't Jack proven that true?)*

It wouldn't work. I knew it immediately, although I didn't write and tell him so for a week. I felt sorry for ruining his Christmas, but after all my heartbreaks, how could I marry someone who couldn't possibly know what a burden a wife in a wheelchair would be?

My reply didn't say "no, never," and Del, convinced God had other ideas, figured a Valentine's Day full moon might persuade me to reconsider.

Oh, the magic of a diamond ring, especially when it is the icing that tops off a most perfect day. The Shumates liked to celebrate Valentine's Day as if it were a holiday next in line after Christmas. I had added to the festivities by decorating the chandelier over the dinner table with red hearts, cupids, and arrows. Jeri's boyfriend, Joe, and Del swelled the ranks of the family for an evening, and laughter filled every corner of the house.

By the time Del got around to popping the question—in person—my resistance had melted. The unseasonably warm day and the moonlight reflected on the lake we had driven to promised the awakening of springtime and caused me to let down my guard momentarily and say yes to life with Del. He assured me that God had brought us together, and when we went home to announce our intentions to Ed and Eleanor, they *knew* God was saying yes to our union.

For several months, Eleanor's insistent encouragement that I should trust God and not lean on my own understanding affected me like coffee: It kept me going as long as she kept refilling my cup. But when her "caffeine" wore off, I knew I had made a big mistake. Although I had expected to marry Jack, I had never really pondered the prospect of being a handicapped wife. But Eleanor was persistent: Didn't I really want the joy and companionship marriage would bring to my life? (*Yes!*) Did I think my petty obstacles too big for God to take care of? (*No.*) Did I not sense that Del was mature enough to handle any problems as they arose?

The night of our engagement, I went to bed at peace that the future was in God's hands. (I was *full* of Eleanor's "coffee.") He had dropped Del in my path. He had pushed Del two steps forward every time Del's fear naturally would have made him take one step back.

Within minutes a contented sleep flooded over me: After all, I was sleeping in the arms of One who understood all my tomorrows.

That spring Del and I loved to stand on the low bridge that crossed the campus's lake and skip flat stones over the glassy surface of the water. Del's muscular arm across the back of my waist allowed me momentarily to lean away from the stone railing and heave the pebbles. What a game it was—again and again trying to see how long I could keep the stones in flight.

No matter how many times the stone jumped or how many feet each leap covered, it always ended its journey on the bottom of the lake. The earth's gravity always won the game. Even so, I tried and tried to see how long I could hold my own against it.

To Del and me it was a silly pastime. But one day in May, Del made an offhand remark about an Old Testament story I had never heard: God, at Elisha's request, made an ax head float. "Here we are," he said, "trying and trying to make tiny stones stay on top of the water, and God could do it at the snap of a finger."

I didn't reply to his comment, but I let the seed of that analogy grow inside my head. For five years I had been spiritually sinking. Hadn't God promised that we would float or even soar, like an eagle? Hadn't God promised?

After a few moments of silence, to which I was growing increasingly more accustomed (Del's and my spoken words to each other were measured), Del quoted a line from a hymn written by Martin Luther: "Did we in our own strength confide, Our striving would be losing."

H'm, I thought. *I wonder what God would do with this stone, with this heart of mine, if I gave Him full rein all the time—not just when Eleanor was around?*

May 30, 1976. That afternoon I gave my heart to Del—for keeps. There's something nice about the phrase holy wedlock and the firm statement: Whom God hath joined together let no one put asunder. At the foot of an altar, God bound me together with His chosen man. I could take no credit for this success. God had played matchmaker despite my dragging feet.

Ed walked me down the left aisle of the small chapel which Del had made his church home. To the strains of Eleanor's organ playing of "How Great Thou Art," Del marched down the right aisle, and we met in front of our friends and family.

The day was perfect—except for the emptiness of the front-row seat, beside Mom.

"Too sick," Dad had said when I had asked if he would come to share in my celebration. I knew he wasn't well. Several months before he had suffered a mild stroke that may have made his reason legitimate. But I wasn't convinced, and my skepticism slightly clouded my day. Inside I wanted to confront his absent face and shake him by the collar. My question or demand hadn't changed much in ten years: "If you loved me, only death itself would keep you away. If you loved me . . ."

But again, I kept my silence. I let the demand sink, like a millstone, to the bottom of my mind, and I pretended that I hadn't noticed his vacant place. I set my eyes on the love of my life and thanked God I had awakened to the amazing grace set down in my path.

9 Voices of Truth Thou Sendest Clear

Wedded bliss. I wonder who invented the phrase. Surely no one who had lived through the first two years of a marriage like mine.

Our days and nights together could better be described as "the best of times, the worst of times."

The full-steam-ahead life of a college campus is worlds away from life in a tract of condominiums. The end of our honeymoon and Del's return to work called a halt to my overflowing schedule but not to my racing motor. I no longer had to prove myself scholastically, now I had to prove myself a good wife.

Those first few years were a blend of the good with the bad, but too often I was my own worst enemy. The spiritual lessons I had chosen not to learn in Emporia had not simply entered my personality through osmosis. The daily lessons had stacked up in front of me and now were entire courses for which I had received either an "incomplete" or a failing grade.

Even before the wedding day, Del and I had felt that having children would be out of the question. Del, especially, felt God's check.

Although I would most probably be able to conceive and deliver a healthy baby, the day-to-day care of a little one would be impossible without full-time or live-in help. We also felt it would be unfair; a child deserved the hands-on care of its mother. I would probably drop a baby that squirmed in my arms. And because house-keeping chores and folding laundry, which most people do easily and with little thought, takes me twice as long as most healthy women, my days, realistically, wouldn't be long enough for the extra work a baby required. On top of my handicap, Del would have a difficult time communicating with a youngster. Del has always noticed a barrier be-tween himself and preschoolers; they do not understand that his heart is with them even though he does not respond to their jabber and attempts at conversation.

God had directed me in the path of His good; I was to be Del's ears and mouth, and Del was to be my feet and stamina. On most days I more than knew that our taking care of each other was joy and responsibility enough for both of us.

But—

Sometimes I felt like a "childless mother." Sometimes nothing less than a baby, my own baby, would satisfy my restlessness. My maternal in-stincts, which were a repressed part of my nature, rumbled through my system. As a young girl I had mothered the newborn puppies of our dachshund who died giving birth to her thirteenth litter. As if they were my own babies, I had gone without sleep to feed the six copper-colored orphans from a bottle, warming them against my ribs, petting them with my fingertips, whispering baby talk in their ears. It was practice, I knew, for the real thing. But the prime years for the real thing were here, and all I had were memories of little dogs that looked like hot dogs and of Mother's own afterthought, Billie, of whom I wished I had taken more care.

I even rationalized my wanting into unselfish terms: I wanted to give Del that gift of life that would be uniquely his, ours—bone of our bones and flesh of our mingled flesh.

The "but" always hit hardest when I would see children from afar who were at their best behavior. And wouldn't you know, it was Del, whom I wanted to make happy, who took the brunt of my want attacks. They started with visions of life at age thirty-five, as I had once thought it would be: I was to be queen of a suburban ranch-style house and owner of a station wagon with wooden side panels and full of children, at least half of whom would be mine.

I couldn't imagine Del being truly satisfied with a wife who was anything short of that image. But here I was, a wife who could manage to dust mop but not vacuum, go along for the ride but not control the wheel, cook dinner and rinse dishes— but only after Del had redesigned and rebuilt the kitchen to put the counters, sink, and range at a midget's level.

Once on this downward spiral, I plummeted like a fireman on a fire-station's pole. Each of my inadequacies added grease to the already slick brass. One cause of restlessness built upon another, ultimately leading to severe depression. "I want to give Del a baby" compounded into "I want to be a good wife" compounded into "I want to be well" compounded, finally, into "I want to be someone I'm not—the someone I used to be."

Escape. I found it in a world that existed only in my mind. My God-made time machine again worked overtime, re-creating happy memories and making them part of the present, not only pieces of the past. To combat the boredom of my housebound existence, I switched to a channel marked high-school star. I not only watched, I played the leading role. To combat eight-to-five housewife loneliness, made more acute by Del's quiet nature, I spent long hours creating lively discussions with my absent mom or airline and college friends.

More than once I got out of bed to get dressed for the day at 4:45 P.M.—in time for Del's arrival home. "Maybe he won't notice that I didn't cook dinner," I thought, fearing the cold tuna platter (again) was a telltale sign of my day's nonexistent activities.

Depression has a way of fueling itself. I was *making* my bad-wife worries into reality.

Del didn't seem to mind the cold dinners; he walked in the door, kissed me hello, and only occasionally commented, "You have such a faraway look in your eye. . . ."

He knew where I had gone but kept his accusations to himself.

But things were even more complicated than I've described. Depression and wishing I were the talk of the city were only half of my inability to deal with life as it really was. The glory of the past may have haunted my days, but its ugliness invaded my nights.

Nothing ever had elated me more than our precious bedroom occasions. However, all nights end with sleep, and Del's presence and tender touch did not ward off a fierce attack of newlywed nightmares. Marriage and its domestic environment triggered scenes from my past to ruin my sleep. There was nothing dramatic about the ghosts' entrance into my dreams. Like actors who are already seated on the stage when a curtain rises in front of them, they—no, it wasn't them, it was *he*—seemed to be in my mind from the minute I nodded off into never-never land. Too often he—Dad—wandered around in my head. At first he was playful and harmless, my old buddy. Then he would turn on me, look at me with disgust, even hate, and then, by his actions and words, deny that I was his daughter. Once the light of his eye, I was cast aside and left to my own isolation.

I don't know if I cried in my sleep. Mother was not sleeping in the next room eager to run to comfort me. Del, although at my side, would not have heard my calls for help.

The terror frequently awakened me. My nightgown would be as wet as if it had just been washed but not dried. My heart would be jumping against my ribs. I would fall back into a fitful sleep until morning, but any day that had been preceded by the horror was a "daymare."

I awoke irritable and usually remained out of sorts all day. If Del went to work, I tried to retreat into my pleasant world of daydreams—anything to separate me from the emotional hellhole into which I was falling. On those days, Del had to put up with my ill-temper only in the evening. But if Dad's image had turned up in my dreams on a weekend night, the sparks between Del and me flew all the next day. He couldn't do anything right.

For instance? Del had a mind of his own when it came to the subject of washing machines. Doing the laundry was difficult for me. The top-loading machine that was in the condo before I moved in was out of reach for me in a sitting position, and the loading was tedious when tried one-handedly. Del had eagerly volunteered to take care of the task. It took him relatively little time, especially since he seemed to just throw the clothes into the barrel. Attempt after attempt for the machine to run a full cycle was thwarted when the irritating buzzer went off, announcing to me (not to Del) that the clothes had not been evenly spread around the agitator.

I was not strong enough or tall enough to untangle and redistribute the wet ropes of clothing and linens. And the blasted bell sent me into an irrational rage. I would pound my fists on top of the dryer and demand that Del do the job correctly. He, on the other hand, refused to admit that uneven spreading was the cause of the problem. It took four years for Del to admit the cause-and-effect relationship; but no amount of stubbornness deserved my day-after-nightmare display of fury.

Scenes such as this were often repeated and exaggerated when Dad began calling me—just to talk. The sound of his voice sent me into a dither, and Del into his private art room—just to get out of my way. Finally, Del lost his patience, sat me down, and made demands—for an explanation. This was no time for a gesturing, lip-reading, or typewritten conversation, but for the real thing, a face-to-face argument with our newly acquired walkie-talkie that amplified sound without giving Del a headache. He sat on one side of the dining table, and I on the other.

"*What* is your problem?" he asked. There was a strange mixture of tenderness and sternness in his voice. "Some days I'm glad I don't hear well, so I don't have to listen to your barrage of pick-pick-pick."

I knew what the problem was, at least the immediate problem. In my mind I could separate my depression from my irritability, and I knew the second was set off only when I was dwelling on Dad. The nightmares frightened me and the phone calls churned them up. I wanted to lash out at anyone who crossed my path, especially any male who got in my way. Yes, I had married Del. Yes, I loved him. Yes, I trusted him. But what *if* he turned on me when he saw how haunted my nights were. The nightmares were my secret. No one but Mom had ever been privy to them, and I hadn't told her the details. The accusations that I had been crazy or hysterical had taken their toll. I hadn't been, and I still wasn't, but I had convinced myself (again) that he wouldn't understand. This had to be *my* secret.

The old family cover-up philosophy had held its ground for nearly a year. He didn't know (or so I thought) of my day-long fantasies or of my nightmares.

"Linda, you're playing games with me. *What* are you hiding?" Del coaxed and prodded until I told him the night's traumas.

He waited for the words that interspersed the sobs and then waited awhile longer before he spoke, insightfully assessing the situation and basing his counsel on the Word he had hid in his heart. It seemed I had no choice but to sit up and take note. "Linda, the resentments and anger you're harboring against your dad are eating you up. Tell me one good thing that is coming from your anger. It's not secretly winning you his approval. It's not effecting any change for the better in him. It's ruining your sleep and my days."

"I can't forgive him. I don't *choose* to dream about him, you know. I can't *choose* to make the past disappear."

Del had other ideas: "But God *commands* us to forgive. I bet Jesus didn't *feel* much like forgiving the soldiers who pounded the nails into His hands, but He did. He was hanging from the cross when He said, 'Father, forgive them for they know not what they do.'"

"He might have been able to say that, but I'm not Jesus."

Again Del caught me up short. "You're right that *you* can't do it. But you forget that Jesus is living in you. Have you even *tried* dumping all your past at Jesus' feet and telling Him that it's all His problem, not yours?"

I had tried that the night I was converted. I had given myself to Him—just as I was. I had desired to become like Him. And maybe I had the afternoon I had found the bourbon glass. Then I had given up a small part of the pain.

"Kind of," I defended myself.

"Dumping it once and then picking it all back up again doesn't work. I have to lay my hurts down in front of Him continually," said Del.

I knew that was true. I had observed and Del had related to me a few of the countless times when he had to choose to turn the other cheek. People were equally or more insensitive to his lack of hearing as they were to my inability to walk. He never received the benefit of any doubt. At least I had had a carefree childhood; in his school years Del had been the target of a garage full of firmly packed snowballs. His grade-school teachers had never taken the time to assess his trouble; he was simply a disciplinary problem they wanted to be rid of. And now—he daily resisted cold shoulders, unintentional though they sometimes were—and *chose* to live on a plane above them.

Del walked into our bedroom and returned with my large brown Bible. "Look at 2 Corinthians 2:5–8," he said, turning to the end of the leather-bound book. "If anyone has caused you grief . . . you ought to forgive and comfort him." Then he turned to Matthew 6 and read words of Jesus: "If you forgive men when they sin against you, your heavenly Father will also forgive you."

Del's sermon did not effect my immediate release from the bondage of my resentments. But several of the points he made peppered my thoughts for days. Jesus' dying words "They know not what they do" seemed apropos. Dad had no conception of the amount of pain he had caused me. The pain only existed in my head, where I held onto it like a monorail train to its track.

Becoming like Jesus (if that's truly what I wanted to do) meant letting go—no longer charging Dad's offenses against him. It meant loving him with God's love.

"He who gains his life must lose it."

Del hadn't specifically pointed out the verse to me, but later that week the words hit me between the eyes. One night after Del had fallen asleep, I, unable to turn off my own mind's motor, had turned on the tape recorder we had strategically placed under the bed and within my reach. I frequently went off to sleep to the sound of Alexander Scourby reading the Word. Since our marriage we had bought a library of Bible and teaching tapes; Del, the spiritual head of our home, had thought it important for me to fill my hours with the encouragement and guidance of the Scriptures. On my good days, the tapes and a local Christian radio station were companionship for me, but more than that, they built up my knowledge of the Lord.

Losing life. Letting go. Did I really have any idea what that meant?

Surely I thought so. Hadn't I lost everything I had once counted on? Hadn't I been humiliated? Stripped of my beauty? Like Lot's wife, hadn't I lost everything? And wasn't I justified in holding my dad responsible for the pain that kept cropping into my head?

"But Linda," the inner Voice asked, "have you ever really let go of the past—all of it—all of the old Linda? Lot's wife lost everything, but letting go was another issue altogether."

Right then and there I couldn't face answering the question, but the next day I laid my thoughts on the table. I told Del where his confrontation had led me—to broader questions and to a dead end. "I don't know *how* to let go of the past—its glory or its pain." I landed my statement, really a plea for help, in his lap and then popped a few of the dozens of daily vitamin pills that had gradually, at Del's suggestion, replaced the Valium.

"Wanting to is the first step," he tenderly explained.

It sounded logical. A part of me had always *wanted* to be like Jesus.

"And I'm not sure one lets go of it all at once and for all time. Remember the verse, 'The just shall live by faith'?"

By faith . . . not by sight.

"By faith one commits the past, present, as well as the future to God's care."

Again he opened the Bible and read aloud just the perfect passage: "Whatever was to my profit I now consider loss for the sake of Christ. What is more, I consider everything a loss compared to the surpassing greatness of knowing Christ Jesus my Lord, for whose sake I have lost all things. I consider them rubbish, that I may gain Christ. . . . I want to know Christ and the power of his resurrection and the fellowship of sharing in his sufferings, becoming like him in his death, and so, somehow, to attain to the resurrection from the dead. . . . I press on to take hold of that for which Christ Jesus took hold of me. . . . Forgetting what is behind and straining toward what is ahead, I press on toward the goal to win the prize for which God has called me heavenward in Christ Jesus" (Philippians 3:7–8, 10–14).

Forgetting what is behind . . . the power of the resurrection . . . by faith . . . they know not what they do . . . to gain, to lose.

Like the sound of a stereo needle stuck on one groove, the phrases repeated themselves in my thoughts, as did images of Lot's wife, whose backward look onto the life taken from her had destroyed her future.

Lot's wife—what was it she didn't want to let go of? The parties, as a younger woman, she had been the life of? The hopes she knew were destroyed? It seems hardly possible she would not have wanted to wash her hands of the pain inflicted on her by the Sodomites. Whatever she was holding on to, didn't she sense the long-term consequences of her grasping, of her last demand for doing things she pleased, for wishing she could be one with the world *and* secure under God's protecting wing?

I didn't want to be Lot's wife.

At dinner the next evening Del made a proposal. "Maybe your letting go of the past would be easier if we symbolically buried it—if we threw out the scrapbooks, the books, and the remembrances of the good *and* bad days that are *over*."

Immediately, I knew what he was asking was of God and, as painful as it would be, necessary—as necessary as Namaan's washing in the Jordan or the Philippian jailer's baptism.

Del continued, "It would be a visible sign of your new commitment. Like putting on a wedding ring is symbolic of a new daily commitment to a spouse."

So after the last bite of our fruit dessert, Del raided the cedar chest in which I had stored the hoarded evidence of my previous life: the scrapbook full of beauty-pageant mementos, the picture album from my first marriage, several extravagant evening gowns, and more frilly nightgowns than I could wear in a lifetime. From the bookshelves covering the far wall of the den, Del pulled

*Voices
of Truth
Thou Sendest
Clear*

paperback novels and self-help books that represented my years of looking in the wrong places for help.

With my tentative approval, Del took charge of the disposal.

As impractical as they were, the clothes were set aside to be taken to the Salvation Army. The books and albums he carried out the front door and down the driveway to the communal dumpster.

Paddling my chair, I followed him into the dark, chilly air. I wasn't *exactly* sure I wanted to go out to the roadside. Would the night engulf me as the dumpster would swallow the papers? Yet an inner "you must" followed by a quiet "by faith" pushed me ahead. If it was my letting go, I would have to take responsibility for the real destruction.

One by one the scrapbooks left my hand and disappeared into the hole. With each thump, I repeated the rather formal relinquishing Del and I had agreed on: "I am giving these to you, Lord, as symbols of my past life. I am trusting that you, who makes all things new, will make my life new. I hereby surrender all my tomorrows to you."

I hoped a wave of cleansing would override the pain of letting go of the person I wanted to be. I hoped my release of the past would begin to erase the pain of the nightmares. If God was asking that I give up the glory of the past, surely He would reduce the agony of the past.

His arms empty of his heavy load, Del pushed me back into the warmth of the house, where I soon fell asleep, nestled under his loving arm.

Both Del and I knew that "exorcising the demons" wasn't the only ingredient of holy living. The bad thoughts we had thrown out had to be replaced with thoughts that were true, noble, right, pure, lovely, admirable, excellent, and praiseworthy.

I got up the next morning, knowing the local Christian radio station would be a lifeline, a help in my trouble. The long, potentially lonely day would have to be pumped full of audible words; I wasn't strong enough to face the hours if they were silent.

Nine o'clock. Ten. Eleven. The clock's hands moved as if they were heavy-laden—slowly enough that I was convinced the day would not end without my lapsing into reveries of escape. The radio sermons only kept half of my attention; the other half . . .

"Where was God, anyway?" I wondered. The radio seemed an artificial substitute for His presence. Was He asking me to buck up and carry this cross of loss all by myself? Was He going to abandon me after I had trusted Him with everything I had?

I struggled until noon to keep the thoughts of the past at bay, but then, I started to sink. My mind rolled back into a partyland I didn't need to be the center of, but which I wanted to watch from the sidelines. Five minutes. Ten minutes. Half an hour. Then the radio sermon I couldn't quite follow ended, and a vocal group flooded the air with an old song that brought me back to the land of the living. The lyrics seemed like a tangible gift from God:

When peace, like a river, attendeth my way,
When sorrows like sea billows roll;
Whatever my lot, Thou hast taught me to say,
"It is well, it is well with my soul."

As the singers repeated that last line several times, the reality of the words settled over me and soaked into me. It *was* well; God was with me. I couldn't hold back the tears that washed away my turbulence and ushered in the contentment that came from knowing He was with me, even smiling at me, giving me a fatherly approval of my big step of faith and encouraging me that He would be at my side when I took each of the baby steps of faith it would take to get me through the forthcoming hours.

He was there—in the room with me.

He wasn't going to abandon me.

I knew He would keep His promise: something beautiful was blossoming in my soul.

Epilogue

With a new dawn, the day after we emptied the cedar chest became history. Another day, then another week was crossed off my calendar.

"One day at a time." The adage almost seems trite; yet its truth is as necessary and relevant now as it was when Jesus reminded His disciples that they should give their attention to the day in front of them, and only that day.

God has been faithful to His promise. For my loss He has given me a life of peace.

He did not take away the nightmares that week, but gradually their intensity decreased, and Del will attest to the fact that their effect on my moods grew negligible. The daydreaming—it also subsided with God's help and by consciously centering my attentions on God and on other people who I realized needed my help. Nothing helps put your own pain in perspective as much as looking at the pain of others and setting your sights on alleviating it.

Together, Del and I set out to counter my

restlessness, boredom, and loneliness with service: An intercessory prayer session became a top priority item on every day's schedule; an interest in African violets grew into a nursery full of potted plants, generation upon generation being propagated and then given away, through our church, to hospitalized and shut-in people (In a way, the violets have become my children); for a year I reviewed new books for a local Christian bookstore (What a profitable way to saturate your mind with the message of the Word); I started writing inspirational poetry that appeared in the church paper; as if he were the student and I the teacher, Del and I worked to improve his enunciation.

The rewards of that have been manifold. In time, shy Del found the confidence to teach small-group Bible classes, first on the Book of Revelation, then on 1 Peter. Of course my opinion is biased, but his gift for teaching, which had been hidden, is exceptional. His years of silent scriptural study have borne fruit in unexpected avenues of service.

The older I get, the more I sit in awe of God's ways. We never know what grace He's planning for tomorrow.

As I finish this book in the waning months of 1983, I celebrate my fortieth birthday. No big parties mark the milestone. A quiet restaurant dinner topped off the rather ordinary day, set near the end of an extraordinary year: My health has greatly improved after several slow years when just getting around the house was a major production. The ups and downs of multiple sclerosis continue their unpredictable cycles, but this, the seventh year of marriage to Del, has been the strongest, physically, of any since I busily buzzed around the Emporia campus. This fall I ventured into teaching a class of women how to be godly wives; I've joined the proofreading staff of the church's various publications. Del and I drove to Topeka for a family reunion—the first time my mother, father, and all my sisters have been together since 1967. Those challenges, along with this chronicling of my journey, would have been impossible a year ago. God has been good in giving me new strength each day.

Is my wishing over? No. But my dreams are now more realistic and future, rather than past, oriented. Along with the apostle Paul, I wish I could go on to my real home. I wish I could run from one end of the gold-paved streets to the other, but I wait (some days more patiently than others), knowing that when God's convinced that my work here is done (Does Del need more years of my care or the church more hours of my prayer, or does my father perhaps need to see a clearer display of the love the Lord has put in my heart for him?), I will be ready to be whisked away.

And then . . . then I know that the well-being of my soul will someday blossom into something more beautiful than words can describe.

Every page of this book
is lovingly dedicated to
my earthly father
and
my heavenly Father,
in hopes that
someday
they will become acquainted.